P9-DZY-245

E169.1
.S593 SLOANE, ERIC
       THE CRACKER BARREL

NORTHAMPTON COMMUNITY
DISCARDED
COLLEGE LIBRARY

NORTHAMPTON COMMUNITY
DISCARDED
COLLEGE LIBRARY

the
Cracker Barrel

Other Books by Eric Sloane

A Reverence for Wood
A Sound of Bells
A Museum of Early American Tools
ABC Book of Early Americana
American Barns and Covered Bridges
American Yesterday
Book of Storms
Diary of an Early American Boy: Noah Blake—1805
Eric Sloane's Almanac
Eric Sloane's Weather Book
Folklore of American Weather
Look at the Sky
Our Vanishing Landscape
Return to Taos: A Sketchbook of Roadside Americana
The Seasons of America Past
An Age of Barns

the CrackerBarrel

by

Eric Sloane

Funk & Wagnalls
New York

Copyright © 1967 by Eric Sloane

All rights reserved.

Library of Congress Catalog Card Number: 67-25419

Printed in the United States of America

ISBN 0-308-70059-7

4 5 6 7 8 9 10

Contents

Author's Note

The old-time country store had a lot more than merchandise. There was a big pot-bellied stove, and a barrel of common crackers within reach of whoever had the time for chatting and a liking for the warmth of a hickory fire. With that kind of surroundings, a fellow could spin yarns or just listen, as well as get to meet everyone in town and hear a lot of different opinions. I knew a store like that, and I can't tell you what I bought there but I do remember most of the stories I heard. "If you listen to them cracker-barrel philosophers," the proprietor would say, "you'll get enough material in a day to fill a book."

Well, I didn't have a book in mind, but when I thought I'd try my hand at doing a newspaper column, I guess my mind went back to the country-store stove, although the title I chose was *It Makes You Think*. The columns have been appearing for a couple of years now, and it seems that a lot of my readers have been clipping them out and pasting them into scrapbooks. Now and then I get a letter urging me to put them in book form, and now and then I have a request from my publisher to do another book. At my age, you can't pass up a combination like that. So, scarcely before I had spent the advance, the book was done.

At first, such a collection of disconnected yarns seemed without sufficient continuity for a book, but there is always use for a bedside "recipe" book that a fellow can pick up to find some food for thought. Therefore, I shall beat the critics by describing the following pages as being incongruous and nothing but a rambling symphony of thoughts and scrap information, no more than you'd pick up at some country store. At least, that's what I hoped it would be.

Eric Sloane
Warren, Connecticut

Foreword

Do I go around painting pictures of fleecy clouds?

Do I sit in the fields painting landscapes?

Do I paint pictures of old red barns, covered bridges, stone fences, haymows, and stuff the like of that?

And do I write books like *Our Vanishing Landscape, A Museum of Early American Tools, A Reverence for Wood,* and *The ABC Book of Early Americana?*

No, I don't!

I am a newspaper columnist and I write a daily column to make a living.

And that's why I'm so damn mad at this Eric Sloane feller.

I don't do what *he* does—so why does he do what *I* do?

You'd think that with all the clouds there are to paint, all the bridges and landscapes to sketch, all there is to write about concerning the days when this country was young—you'd think that would be enough for this Sloane.

But, no. Oh, no! He's got to do more than that.

He's got to invade my field—and, s'help me—write a column! And then, alas, compound it by putting his columns in a book.

Like as if there ain't enough columnists in the business today, all of them starving and scratching around for ideas and borrowing money from relatives and staving off creditors, and the bank, and the Internal Revenue Service.

So now we have yet another hungry mouth in our field. Another competitor, another conniving chronicler scrambling for the few pennies available to us columnists.

I am a syndicated columnist, distributed by United Feature Syndicate to newspapers in sixty-six cities. But it has taken me four years to achieve this.

Sloane started his wretched little column, I dunno, maybe a year ago, and already his scheming and his silver-tongued appeals to editors have built his string up to like about a dozen papers. There's no telling how far he'll go! And I'm just waiting for the day when he snitches the first paper away from me! On that day, I swear, I'm gonna get me an airplane and go up and start painting clouds!

I've got to admit that this guy is good—for a neophyte—and that his column "It Makes You Think" really lives up to its title. Sloane, for instance, is likely to give you tips on how you can win bets from friends.

"If," he said in one column recently, "you ever see lightning from the South or the East (anywhere but from a Westerly quadrant), you can bet that the storm will miss and pass you by. That's because concentrated storms move in an Easterly direction."

Sloane also tells you about fascinating things like: the Franklin stove that we know is *not* a Franklin stove, the Dutch oven that we know is *not* a Dutch oven, the hourglass hardly ever measures exactly one hour, and there's no such thing as the Pennsylvania Dutch (they're really Germans).

Now, how the hell can the rest of us columnists beat stuff like that?

Most of us don't know enough to come in out of the rain—let alone tell which way a storm will travel.

And that's why, here and now, I'm going to show you what I might just do to get even.

Here's the kind of thing I might well turn to:

by NORTON MOCKRIDGE

That's a barn.
(Just thought I'd better let you know.)

New York City
June, 1967

the CrackerBarrel

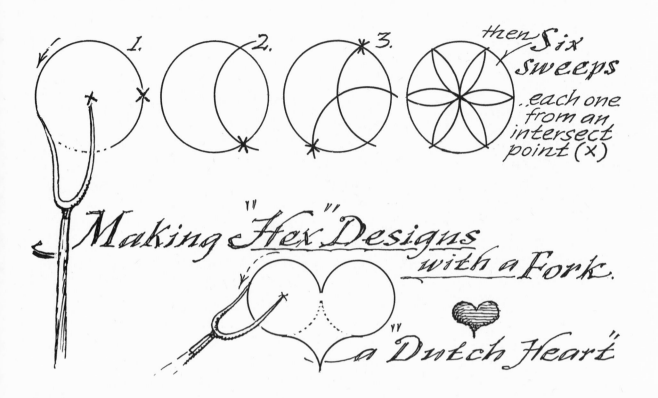

1. 2. 3. then six sweeps ..each one from an intersect point (x)

Making "Hex" Designs with a Fork.

"a Dutch Heart"

Norton Mockridge is partly responsible for this column-writing adventure in a way, for while I have a memory full of cracker barrel stuff, I've always wondered how a daily columnist manages to collect sufficient material. I quickly learned from Norton the habit of keeping a pad and pencil nearby—even by my bedside. With a few rich dreams, I found, one can run out of paper before daylight. If you dine with Norton, whose wife puts a pad and pencil alongside his regular place-setting, you observe that he does more scribbling than eating. One time he left a restaurant table and disappeared into the men's room, came back only to pick up his pad, and disappeared again. "I got some swell material," he said when he finally returned. "When you start your own column, don't overlook graffiti."

Graffiti (scrawlings on walls or other alluring surfaces) suddenly took on a new importance in my pursuit of Americana, and so in honor of Norton's encouragement to intrude on his source of livelihood, I thought I should present a few of my own graffiti discoveries.

The old covered bridge portals were always crowded with designs and scribblings and messages; some, carved right into the wood, have withstood the passing years' toll. One example is a fine arrow-pierced heart carved into the old Gaylordsville (Connecticut) covered bridge with the inscription "Eddie Loves Edith"; some smart aleck had added "At Least Once a Week," which someone else (Edith herself?) had done her inadequate best to erase.

You can still find early schoolroom desks in antique shops, and many include graffiti like "Mary Is a Pip" or "Lucy Has a Beau." One had "Teachers Pet" carved into it, followed by "So Do Students."

Some of America's longest-lasting graffiti were the work of itinerant sign painters whose occasional piety—"Prepare To Meet Thy God" and "God Is Love," for example—can be found inscribed on flat rocks along the highways. One rock, with "Stop and Repent" painted on it, rolled down into the middle of a road near Brattleboro (Vermont), and for about a year travelers, apparently thinking it was a religious monument, simply detoured around it, often saying a short prayer or crossing themselves.

It took me a while to learn that those strange chalk or painted markings on telephone poles were put there by the advance agent of some circus. They have a code all their own: by arrows and letters they warn against sharp turns, bad hills, belligerent policemen, unfriendly villages; they mark speed traps with ST and recommend diners with good coffee by a J (for Java). And by a lot of other symbols they make the circus caravan's trip safer and more interesting.

There's graffiti in the old barns too, done, I suppose, on work-slow rainy days. In one a long-gone farmhand complained, "I Hate Cows." A lot of the Pennsylvania "Dutch" barns have folklore graffiti and hex designs scratched into their walls—if you look closely you can see that they were the work of two-pronged hay forks, which make excellent compass markers. Now and then, high enough in a barn's hayloft to conjure up all kinds of romantic suppositions, you find hearts-and-initials carved into the beams. I remember best the heart-and-initials in an ancient barn sold by a century-old widow in Maine. "I'll sell the barn," she said, "but there's one beam in it I want to keep." The barn was torn up for lumber, but that one beam was saved.

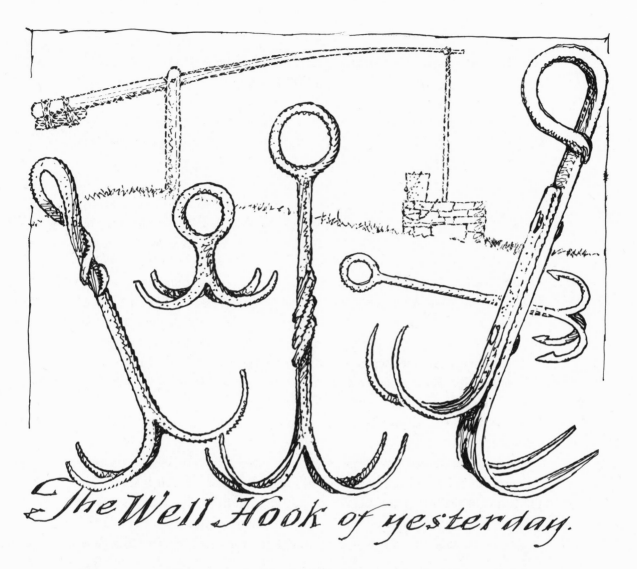

The Well Hook of yesterday.

My pet raccoon Button-nose had been missing for a week. And then one night, when I went past one of the ancient wells of my farmhouse, I decided to investigate the water level. It is only at night, and with a flashlight, that you can really see into such a well. But Button-nose had been curious too, and evidently had beaten me to it a week before. There he was, his body floating about ten feet down in the well.

If you have ever tried to fish a dead animal from a well, you will know the difficulties. But my old tool museum has in it a number of well-hooks or "grapnels" made for just such an occasion, and one of them served its purpose nicely. They were all sold to me by antique shops who said they were meat-hooks, but from research I knew better. Meat, I learned, was usually hung on wooden spikes or it was hung from stationary hooks by a rope. All those three- or four-pronged hooks you see in antique shops, I learned, are well-hooks. Why then, should people need so many well-hooks?

The answer is that before refrigeration, the dug well was used for much more than drinking water. Pails and series of pails were often lowered into the well, filled with food that needed to be cool during the summer months. And there was always a pail or something falling into the well. Sometimes you would grapple for something and even lose the grappling hook, so you'd need another hook to get the lost one. At any rate, because there was no way to see into the well below the water's surface, wells were often "hooked" every day just to make sure there were no dead beasties or other things down there in the darkness.

Antique buffs are just beginning to collect these ancient hand-wrought hooks, and it is interesting to note how many kinds of hooks there used to be. We are told how people used to hang baskets of fruit from the ceiling as well as meats and herbs (for drying), but the early houses had very low ceilings and I don't think people fancied bumping into a ham every now and then. Those hooks you often see in the ceilings of early homes were not for food at all, but for Saturday nights. If you put poles on them, and then hung blankets from the poles, you would find that you had made a nice tent-house around a fireplace, just the thing for the privacy and warmth of a wooden-tub bath. I have often told people this, and then they showed me that their ceiling hooks were not around any fireplace. But a little detective work and evidence of a hearth on the floor disclosed that indeed there had been a fireplace under the hooks at one time.

I shall always remember a friend to whom I told this story, who later came by hard times. He couldn't pay his oil bill and he was faced with living in his old house for the winter without central heating. But he made use of his ceiling hooks, forming a blanketed room around the main fireplace, where he had a bed, a chair, and even a TV set. Feeling sorry for him, I visited him one night during the coldest time of the year, but the roaring fire and the comfort of confinement had such appeal that when I made ready to leave, I actually envied him.

Some day I'll learn where the phrase "playing hooky from school" came from: I've traced it back to 1848 without even a hint. But I did learn where the phrase "hook or crook" came from. I found it in a really ancient lease. "Tenants must not rob my lands of good wood," it read, "excepting dead limbs from the trees, such as can be pulled down by ordinary hook or crook."

the Full Measure

When some of your favorite, familiar things begin to appear in the antique shops, you know you've reached maturity. I wince when I see those bent wire "ice-cream-parlor chairs" displayed as early Americana, for I remember when an ice-cream soda was something special, and the sundae was something brand new.

Ice-cream sodas were once considered so big and sloppy that "Sunday go-to-meeting clothes" were protected in some cities by an actual law against serving sodas on the Sabbath. Then confectioners left out the splashy soda and put more manageable syrup in its place, inventing the "Sunday" or "Sundi." That soon became popular and they made it look French by spelling it "sundae," and finally—by making it big and messy—it became a symbol of the American full measure.

The ice-cream soda is still a full-measure symbol, not considered a true soda unless the foam is running over the rim, with the ice cream balanced on top, and a dab of whipped cream just for daring; then it is slid across the marble counter-top to you, like an outboard in a choppy sea, leaving a wake of slosh behind it. The sundae is still ridiculous, particularly those roadside portable jobs that consist of a Matterhorn of pseudo ice cream, with a soggy avalanche of syrup that runs down and over your fingers. Just to prove they can't put anything else on it, they shower the mountain walls with shredded nuts and top the peak with a cherry. Boy, that's living!

Another example of American full measure is evidenced in our national cup of coffee, which isn't complete without a saucer to catch the overflow. Every time you lift the cup, the saucer drippings fall in a nice pattern onto your lap. On my way to town recently, I stopped at a diner. "What I want," I said "is half a cup of coffee." (That I find, leaves room for the "cream.")

All the customers stopped eating to look at me, and it took the waitress a moment to compose herself. "We don't serve no half cups," she said. "Only full cups."

"Well, I'm a customer and what I want is half a cup. I intend to pay you for a full cup. I also intend to tip you."

That stumped her for an instant, and the other customers waited for her reply. "That wouldn't be fair to you," she said. "We don't wish to cheat people. You pay for a full cup, you get a full cup. Then you can drink only half of it. OK?" The customers nodded approval as she moved toward me with a pot of coffee.

She poured out a cup of coffee that flowed over the rim and into the saucer. "That," she said, "is an honest cup of coffee." More nodding from the other customers.

"I am sure you are honest," I replied, "but if you will please pour out half of this mess and give me a dry saucer, I will be most pleased."

By now the customers had forgotten their eating completely and sat waiting for the next act. "We don't want no trouble here, mister," she said. "You have your coffee the way we serve it. Maybe you'd like for me to call my husband?"

It didn't seem worth the bother to continue the comedy, so I left and waited till I reached the city for my coffee. There, they give me my half cup automatically. But, alas, that morning there was a new waitress on hand. I heard the chef whisper to her as I sat down, "Give that gentleman half a cup of coffee. He's from England or something."

The American habit of giving more than enough is most generous and impressive, but I do think if we must make a religion of generosity, it might be better to favor quality more than quantity. A half cup of coffee will aways bring the sharpest complaint, but I have yet to see someone send back any coffee as being inferior. The housewife will buy cookies with artificial flavoring, make-believe fruit, and about as much nourishment in them as in the cardboard container. But let there be only eleven cookies instead of the advertised twelve, and watch out for an irate housewife. She'll even write her Congressman.

Wheel- *Barrow.*
C.1875

Hand barrow c.1700
the wheel (x) came later.

If they made wheelbarrows the way they used to, I'd have bought one at the nearest store, but the fact is that I went a hundred miles (all the way to Pennsylvania) to get an antique 1875 wheelbarrow. That sounds pretty ridiculous, but some men like mustaches and I happen to like wheelbarrows. Mustaches get into your coffee while wheelbarrows are utilitarian, so if you are a reader with a mustache, just don't be quick to criticize me.

There's something personal about a wheelbarrow. You can't, for example, use a wheelbarrow with another person. Just have a friend take one handle while you take the other, and the result will surprise you: it just won't work. Working with the wrong wheelbarrow is like wearing an ill-fitted suit.

When you live in the country, you should have certain things—like a station wagon and a good stout cane and a tweed coat with suede patches on the elbows. But above all, you must always have a sturdy wheelbarrow. Whether for carrying sod or firewood or gardening equipment, there is no other way but with a good old-fashioned wheelbarrow. At the moment I have three modern barrows as well as my newly acquired antique, and I also have a bump on my head. The bump is the result of trying to carry a load downhill in a most modern, deluxe, pneumatic-tired wheelbarrow. My undersized ten-inch wheel encountered a ten-inch depression and I did a ten-foot arc in midair over said vehicle.

I am certain that everyone using modern wheelbarrows is constantly annoyed at those small toy wheels which sink into the slightest hole. But my hardware man says we live in an age where we "have to take what we can get" and "we can't fight City Hall." I think both of these statements are un-American and completely disgraceful. And that's why I went to Pennsylvania for a properly wheeled barrow that I can use without courting disaster and in which I can carry my apples without joggling them into applesauce.

The tiny wheel problem has gone unnoticed for a long while, so allow me to present it as I see it. In the early days, wheels had to be big because the roads were rough. Wagons and other vehicles could go through forests or over bad roads with very little trouble because of their enormous wheels. Even the early automobiles had big wheels. But except for the low pressure and wider circumference of the modern tired wheel, the new tiny automobile wheel (often smaller than regular motorcycle size) is much less efficient than the old Model T sized wheel! In the first place, your new wheel turns more times to get from here to there; therefore it logically wears out more rubber—the same quality of present-day rubber on a large wheel would last twice as long. Second, the ride would be better: a small wheel has to ride into and out of a small hole that a large wheel could go right over. Finally, a larger circle offers more ground traction so that a small wheel gives less braking surface and is more liable to skid.

The automobile experts will not argue with all this, and they do admit that the small wheel is mostly the product of styling. The only real advantage of a small wheel is to get the car lower to the ground, but we seem to be already too low for proper vision. (If you get on your *knees* in the road alongside the driver of the average full-size car, your eyes will be on the same level or lower than his!)

If you have ever wondered why the biggest trucks can pass you so artfully with a full load at eighty miles an hour, remember the truckdriver's benefit of wheels that are turning much slower. He also has more traction area needed for braking and control. The big truck's superiority on the highway is due mostly to its huge wheels. It's also why you'll find the world's fastest racing cars using oversize wheels. So I'm sold on big wheels and, darn it all, a fellow *can* fight City Hall. Or buy antique wheelbarrows.

the American Neck-tie

One of the world's strangest customs is found in the country where all the male inhabitants are required to wear a ribbon tied around their necks. If discovered without this identifying ribbon, they are regarded as improperly dressed. In case you don't know, the name of this country is America, and the ribbon is called a necktie.

Those dinner invitations that end with "black tie" were first planned just to let you know it wasn't "white tie" or formal; but those were the days when people dressed properly for occasions. I suppose some day you'll see dinner invitations ending with just the word "tie." And you'll even find men refusing to go because they'd have to wear one.

One of the best things that has ever happened to the American male, in my opinion, has been the sweat shirt. That isn't a good name for any garment; it seems they could have called it a perspiration blouse, at least. But what I like about it most is that you don't have to wear a necktie with it. One stubborn restaurateur said I couldn't enter his place in a sweat shirt. "I'm sorry," he said, "but it is a steadfast rule—you must have a necktie." So I went out to my car, where I always have a kit of paints, and I painted down the front of my shirt a nice big polka-dot tie. That left the fellow speechless and it won me entrance to the place, although I must admit he gave me a table way over in the corner next to the men's room.

Once I spent the day as a witness in court, and it was interesting fun picking out the good guys and the bad guys. Funny thing though, how all the bad guys were the ones without a necktie. Of course, the judge and the court clerk and the lawyers were nicely ribboned, and it made me think about that strange American symbol, the necktie. It isn't a garment and it isn't just a decoration, but it is certainly a national necessity, so I guess you have to call it a symbol.

Before there was such a thing as the necktie (in the 1700's) the term "necktie party" or "necktie social" was frequently used to describe a lynching. So the word necktie must first have been used in ridicule, for something that looked like a hangman's knot. Before the necktie actually reached the dictionary however, that reference only listed the "neckcloth" and, up until the mid-1800's, men wore neckcloths.

Some restaurants in New York have a number of different size coats for men who forgot to bring their coats or who wanted to dine coatless. They also have neckties for those who forgot to wear ties. One time I recall seeing a man who was refused entry to the Biltmore Hotel dining room because he had no tie, but the situation was fixed when he removed one of his shoelaces and tied that in a bow around his collar.

But my most embarrassing situation resulted one hurried morning when I forgot to flap down the collar of my shirt after having put on my necktie. Feeling the collar brush against my face, I thought I had not put a tie on, and absentmindedly tied another one right on top of the first one. After a cocktail at luncheon that noon, my lady guest eyed me sadly. "So you've had your little joke," she said, "and I didn't think it a bit funny."

"I haven't the slightest idea of what you are talking about," I said.

"Of course you know," she replied, "that you have two neckties on."

I've often wondered what became of that girl; I never saw her again.

Small size Americana

It may come as a surprise for some of us to find that the average early American was slight of build and rather short. I have a collection of beaver-skin top hats and some three-corner-style ones that go back to the Revolutionary days. And not just some, but every single one of them, sits on top of my head like a peanut. Over at the Whaling Museum in Mystic, Connecticut, there are a lot of interesting exhibits, but what seems to impress people more than anything else are the tiny bunks in the old whaling ship. Even during the Civil War days we hadn't really begun to spread out yet and, if you inspect the old wartime uniforms, you might think we had armies of midgets. There are early antique chairs and rockers that are so tight a fit for modern rumps that they are being sold as "children's chairs." There's no doubt about it, the early American was more trim-waisted and small-bottomed than we are today. But then they hadn't started eating that modern white bread that builds you up in twelve ways.

Benjamin Franklin said he'd never seen a fat farmer. But as small as the old-time fellows were, they were all wiry strength. Now hear the interesting part:

the average early heart was the same size as the heart of today. So you can see that the modern heart has a bigger job to do—pumping more blood to a bigger body, and a longer distance.

Perhaps it is significant that the only early invention that is completely American seems to be the rocking chair. And ever since its creation, we have specialized in the art of sitting. We ride in a sitting position to work in the morning, and then sit at a desk all day. We ride on our bumpkins back home again, where we sit at dinner and manage to try out our legs only from the table to the TV, and there we fall asleep still resting on our same said end. Our idea of sports is much too often sitting and watching others enact the sport, so that the average man spends about ninety percent of his waking hours on his behind. Our poor spines have become strings of bones where the heads sit on one end and we sit on the other. Man has long been separated from the other animals as "the one who walks on two legs" yet, as we really sit so much more of the time, perhaps we should be called the "sitting animal."

And have you noticed women's seats lately? Well, if you have neglected such research, I can enlighten you. While men have done more sitting, women do their housework on their feet, and the American female bottom has become smaller and trimmer while most men in their later years have become back-heavy. You might recall the actress of a century or so ago—her claim to fame was always her wavy bulges. Our present-day Audrey Hepburn or her type wouldn't have got to first base in those days; they would have been sent to an institution to fatten them up.

Men are definitely becoming physically inferior to women. Their mortality rate was ten percent higher than that of women in 1920; by 1950 it had become sixty-eight percent. This is said to be the result of hard work and worry, but people do not die naturally from overwork. Also, the average man's work is more varied and exciting, while less physical, than that of a mother and housewife, so it just might be that man is actually sitting himself to death. Those new style tight pants for men might have some advantage after all: they might tend to keep a fellow from sitting down too much.

Candy, the stuff that evolved into a multi-billion-dollar industry more responsible than anything else for decayed teeth in America, isn't really all bad, because it makes work for a lot of people—including the pediatricians and dentists. But the way we regard candy as part of the daily diet and national nutrition leads one to believe that candy has been with us for a long while. Not so however, for even after the Civil War period, candy was only a verb in the dictionary, meaning "to boil fruits in syrup and conserve them." The early American settlers used maple syrup for kitchen sweetening and imported loaf-sugar came a bit later, but candy, as we know it now, was completely unknown. The great American candy bar is less than a hundred years old!

Above, you may see a pair of *candy-scissors* and a *candy-hammer*. They were used long ago to break loaf-sugar into edible chunks. But "candy" at that time was direct from the Sanskrit *khanda* meaning "a broken piece," so the word candy-scissors only meant "scissors for breaking anything into little pieces."

Served at dinner for dessert, a chunk of loaf-sugar was placed on the table with scissors and hammer, and passed around. That sounds like the birth of the candy bar, but it is a much more complicated story than that. I beg your patience.

The candy that we know today evolved from the very early bakeshop. It seems that bakers were often asked to make sweetmeats (small, sweet cakes) for special occasions like Christmas or Easter or New Year's or birthdays, and they created wooden molds for appropriate shapes and designs. The first such cake was for New Year's Day (which came in March at that time), so they called those sweetmeats "March Pan" and then "Marchpane" or "New Year bread." I told you it was going to be complicated, didn't I? When Italy started making marchpane sweetmeats, they didn't say "marchpane" very well and what came out was *marzipan*. They didn't have maple sugar either and they used too much native almond paste, so that "Italian marzipan" we know so well is nothing but a mispronunciation and mistaken recipe for our own early Marchpane.

By the end of the 1700's, most bakeshops had gathered so many wooden Marchpane molds and did such a fine business with their holiday sweetmeats that they opened separate rooms called confectionery departments. Most everyone made their own bread anyway, and few households owned wooden marchpane molds. Some of the old molds can still be bought in antique shops, but almost every one you can find came from overseas. The American ones are made of applewood, walnut, or other native woods, and if you find one it is worth ten of the European molds. I made the mistake of starting a collection, even trying to duplicate the maple-sugar-and-dough mixture and making my own Early American marchpane.

I say mistake, because whenever a guest sees the molds hanging on my living room wall, they feel compelled to say, "What are those—cookie molds?" Of course the answer takes exactly as long as it took you to read this, by which time my guest has lost interest and gone to another room, leaving me still mumbling Marchpane history (to myself).

When the Civil War ended and just about all handmade things were doomed by stock metal copies, the wooden mold disappeared. It was then that our country-store "penny candy" came into being, in the form of chocolate babies, banana shapes, Foxy Grandpas, and orange slices. And to the betterment of the sugar industry and the detriment of teeth and waistlines, the American candy bar was born.

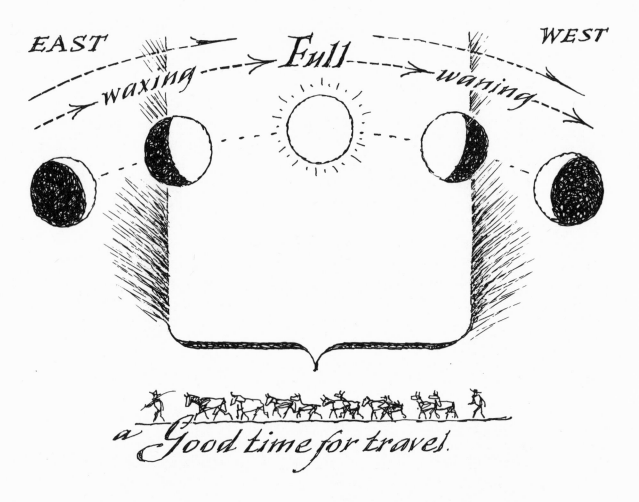

waxing —→ *Full* —→ *waning*

a *Good time for travel.*

You'll still find people who think the early American almanack was some sort of mystical weather predictor. And many of the new editions of the almanack actually do make a stab at weather prediction (just because they think they are supposed to do just that). But the old-time almanack was simply an amusing and educational calendar. Merely incidental are the occasional weather hints gleaned from recordings of what happened on certain dates the year before.

As for superstition in the almanacks, you can read into the wording just about whatever you want to. I'll give you a classic example. In the very popular *Old Farmers Almanack* in 1963 (if you still have one), turn to page 31 (November) and read the monthly watchword at the bottom of the page; it tells how this will be "a month to guard against crime." Now look at the entry for November 22: "Night is coming on," it reads, "and murder. Has not half the world been murdered?" That, of course, was the day that President Kennedy was assassinated. The watchword goes on: "No, nothing in this world has been murdered—nothing that cannot live again." And then it quotes one of Kennedy's favorite lines: "Havoc, havoc is just a cry. Give the best of yourself always—just to living—but for others, if you can."

[17]

You almost can hear the almanack saying ". . . not what your country can do for you but what you can do for your country." And if you are a superstitious almanack buff, you'll swear that this was a prediction.

Even the old-time hints about the best phases of the moon for going to town or for planting things or for shingling a roof—these aren't the least bit tainted by superstition. As for going to town or shingling a roof, these were things usually done by moonlight in those days. The trip to town with a drove of cattle often took two or three days and the actual traveling was done as much at night as possible, so you certainly wanted the longest and brightest moonlight, because no one had yet invented the flashlight. You seldom shingled a roof in the day during summer because it was too hot, and besides, there were too many other things to be done. A full moon and the coolness of night made roofing a cinch. As for planting overground and underground vegetables during certain moon phases, science is still at odds about the outcome, but several tests have shown proof that the old-timers were absolutely right. As to the times for cutting down trees those moon dates were simply methods of dating the season: the farmer didn't carry a calendar with him but there was always the moon at hand to give him a date. And if you think it was superstition instead of science about the right time to fell a tree, just regard the stuff our modern lumberyards give you; they fell trees any old time, with or without sap-run, and the warps show it.

Poor Great-great-grandfather was a lot more scientific than we give him credit for, and he really frowned on superstition much more than we do now. We still hang up a "lucky horseshoe" and we take it pretty seriously. "Never hang one with the prongs downward because that will always let the luck fall out." But let the old-timer decorate his beloved barn with some original decoration and we call it a "hex sign" used to frighten away the bad spirits. Of course, when his wife made exactly the same designs on a quilt, we were more polite and allowed they were just primitive folk-designs. You know—like modern Pop Art.

Slow but sure.

The old-timers had an astounding way of doing things slowly but getting the most work done. If you've ever seen an expert using a cradle-scythe, you'll know what I mean. He'll look as if he's falling asleep, but at sundown you'll find him going at the same pace and just as strong as when he began.

Ben Franklin said it well:

> The slowest beasts are always strongest
> And manage, too, to live the longest.

Some folks rush through life so, they give the impression they want to get it over with as soon as possible. Speed is all right if you want to get somewhere in a hurry, but man's fascination for speed just for the sake of speed seems pretty foolish. The late speed pilot Malcolm Campbell didn't want to go any-where in particular; he just wanted to see how fast he could do it, and that seems to be a useless aim and a waste of one's life. It certainly was of his.

Going fast is an art, but going slowly is an art too, for the trip itself is often more fun than when you get there. One of the most popular treats in the old days, when they excelled in the art, was the Albany Night Boat from New York, and the best part of it was that it went so slowly. Naturally you never made the trip alone, but the excursions were responsible for some of the happiest marriages. It just points out one of the merits of going slowly; you can miss a lot of fun by trying to get anywhere in a hurry.

Time savers have become an obsession in America, with everything from electric toothbrushes to shoeshiners, and even a gadget that can cook a three-minute egg in two minutes. No one thinks twice about what to do with the time saved. Perhaps you should just work harder to pay for the time-saving gadgets.

The old-timers had a lot of sayings about the art of slowness, but I've yet to hear one about speed. "If it's a quick decision you want," they said, "the answer is always no." "The fastest operator," said the almanack, "will turn out to be the most successful and most popular and richest fellow in the grave-yard." Every farmer knew that "the fastest grown pumpkin always turns out to be the poorest."

I have an older brother who learned as a child to chew each mouthful thirty-three times. He read that in a magazine and he thought it was a pretty good idea. The only trouble with it, however, was that it was too obvious and the whole family used to watch him and count right along. Now most of my family has died of ulcers and worry, but brother George is still chewing.

So you see there are points of merit in slowness and, although they don't always favor more money in the wallet, they do favor a richer, fuller, longer, and smoother life. When I learned to fly, my first lesson was in the art of slow maneuvering: the best turns were the smooth slow ones—the ones that strained the plane were the quick ones. And the faster you go, the easier and slower you must control a maneuver.

So I want to start a new fad of American science to keep up with the jet set. I want to introduce the art of slowness. Remember "go-go?" I'll call mine "slow-slow." Think how much more we shall see. Think how much money we can save. Think how many lives could be spared. Think how much more time we'll have just to think, and maybe how many wars we can stay out of. Let's be all for rockets and spaceships going faster and faster. That's what they're for. But let's give a little thought to the great and gentle art of going slowly.

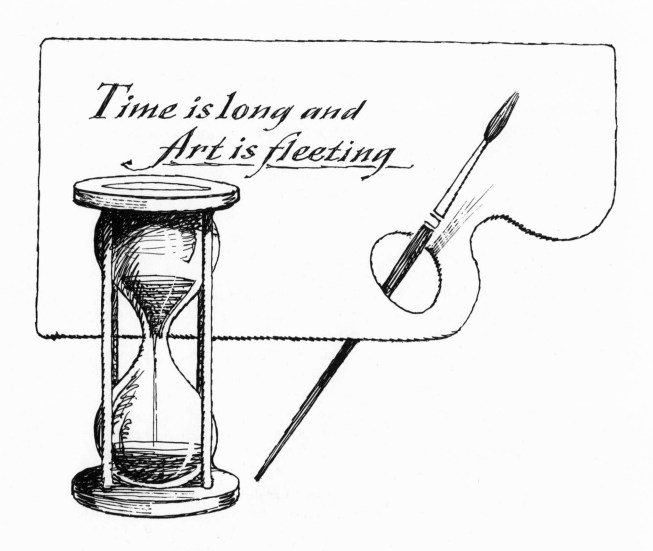

Time is long and
Art is fleeting

Time actually stands still; it is we who do the passing.

My column written about the "gentle art of going slowly" brought in a lot of critical letters from the jet set. So I want to state that I'm fully aware that there's such a thing as going *too* slowly and, just to please everyone and give the opposition equal time I'd now like to say a few words about "the fine art of going fast."

They say that to put your personality into your handwriting, it is necessary to write with a good fast swing. I go along with that. The slow people are seldom the "personality people," anyway. Just to demonstrate that point, try to write your name, giving yourself a full minute to do the job. When you've finished, you'll find that it isn't your signature anymore; it's lost all its personality. It looks like a complete forgery.

Painting is that way too. The Sunday painter who tries hard to be good and careful and exact is his own worst enemy. Even knowing when to stop is a fine art. At one time I knew a famous artist whose work breathed personality. He did simple sketches of fashionable ladies and gentlemen and his clean, quick strokes made you feel his genius. His method might interest you. He worked for a long while (often a full week) in preparation. He did sketches and tracings until they overflowed his desk and lay scattered on his studio floor. Then, one day when he was confident that he knew just what he wanted to do, he calmed himself with a cup of coffee and then sat in a relaxed position. And with a sure hand, he did the sketch he'd worked on all week—in about three minutes. The result was always breathtaking.

Any good artist will tell you that of every dozen pictures done, the best one nearly always happens to be the one done in the least time. Yet the worst mistake he can make is to tell you about it. It should be his secret, because people like to think the job well done takes the longest time to do. I remember one of the best paintings I ever did that sold for a top price. It wasn't the price that makes me remember, however. When the buyer asked me how long it took to paint his picture, I answered him honestly (about six hours) and he changed his mind about the painting and about me too. He's never spoken to me since.

The old problem of answering the question, "How long did it take you?" is almost as important to a painter as learning how to mix paints, for he will be asked that of everything he paints for the rest of his life. Whistler came up with a model answer when a buyer sued him for overcharging. "It took me a lifetime," he replied. Or you might reply that it took you thirty years to do it in two hours. Another good reply is, "None of your business," but that doesn't make many friends.

One time two visitors stopped by my studio while I did a painting that just happened to take me about an hour to do and, fortunately, I knew when to stop. "You mean it's completely done?" one of them asked.

"One hour for a painting," said the other in a whisper, "is eight paintings a day! And fifty-six paintings every week!"

The other visitor took out a pad and pencil and started scribbling something. "Why that's nearly three thousand paintings a year!"

"Take your time and do it well" is perhaps the most time-worn piece of advice, but it doesn't pertain to creative work. Paul Revere said to his apprentice, "A slow person makes me nervous. It makes me want to take over and do the job for him." And no doubt Paul Revere was an expert at being fast. If he wasn't, how could he have crowded into one lifetime a mastery of the arts of bell-founding, boiler-making, metalcraft, printing, politics, design and manufacture of currency, silversmithy, architecture, industrialism, cannon-making, boat-building, copper-roof manufacture, gunpowder manufacture, and cartooning. Oh yes—he was fast on a horse, too.

*You can spot the old ones
a mile away*

If you would try to define the difference between the house of one or two centuries ago and the house of today, you must not include inventions such as plumbing and picture windows: the real difference is aesthetic and more basic than mere innovations. You can motor along an old road at late sunset and, just by the silhouettes of the houses, spot the old ones a mile away. Even the so-called antique reproductions won't stand that test. I've tried to define this difference, and I think I've run it down.

Great-grandfather decided upon a shape first, and then he arranged rooms within that shape—nowadays we decide upon the rooms and then arrange them into a shape. If you'll look at the floor plans of most of our modern split-level ranch houses you'll see what I mean; the simplest design is usually an L-shape, but the more complex ones branch out, octopuslike. Then look at the outside bulk of any ancient house and you'll see simplicity and character molded together into a wonderfully identifying shape.

In so many ways the Civil War was the turning point for America, and it was this short era that changed the old into the new way of our house building. Houses built during that chaotic period look, indeed, like houses built during a chaotic period. The stark, simple, primitive, individual lines of colonial building became lost almost overnight, and the overdone, pretentious, decorated, "citified" look took over.

Another difference between the house of today and the house of before the Industrial Revolution, is that the old house had a strong skeleton, as any body ought to have. And then the skin was stretched over the skeleton. Now, however, the skeleton is softwood one-and-a-half inches by three-and-a-half (erroneously called two-by-fours), while the skin of plywood and clapboards is usually stronger than the skeleton. You can't even buy the old-time skeleton timbers of ten-by-ten or twelve-by-twelve.

Builders will tell you that modern buildings are just as strong as the old ones, but if you can recall some of those aerial photos of a modern housing development after a tornado went through, you will remember a flat area of rubble. There have been tornados that struck the old houses and took off their "skin," but the massive skeleton timbers always held. In the old days, there was such a man as a "framer" and the rest of the work was done by plain builders and carpenters. The framer is no more.

Another difference between the old and new houses, of course, is the difference between wooden pegs and nails. And somehow or other, people still insist that wooden pegs were used because of a shortage of nails. Even if the old-timer had all the nails in the world, he would never have thought of fastening framing together with them. Wherever you did that, you'd soon find splits, rust, and rot. Even today, you find all window frames and fine carpentry using wooden pegs because nails are inferior. Most wooden trunnels (tree-nails) were inserted heated and dry, so that they would swell up and weld the joint together. Often the trunnel hole would be slightly offset, so it would take hard hammering to force the trunnel through.

There are a lot of differences between the old and the new in house building, and the differences too frequently involve quality and conscience and lastingness, those three vanishing requisites in a good house.

Art is how you look at it.

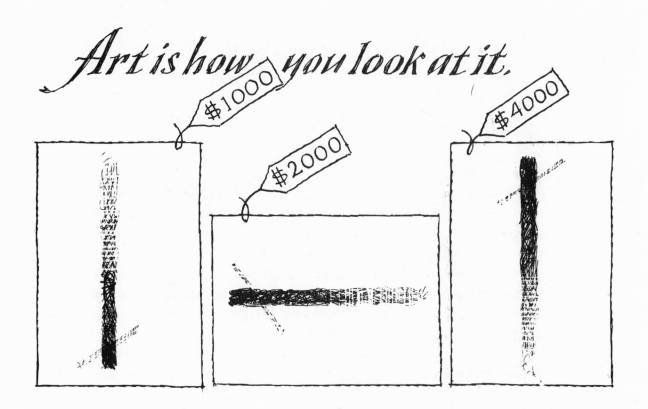

Hardly a day goes by that someone doesn't say, "What do you think about Modern Art?" One time I was asked my opinion of "Pop Art" and I thought a suitable reply might be "Wam, zam, sock, and pow!" I don't know what that means either but it seemed to satisfy. "That's just the way I feel about it," said the man.

If modern art has nothing else, it certainly has a sense of humor. Recently I found myself viewing a big white canvas with a red smear on it in that New York museum that looks like a huge modernistic cement toilet bowl. The frame was costly and so was the museum; I'm sure I must have been wrong but all I could see was a big white canvas with a red smear on it. Then I became aware of another person beside me, also looking at the thing. We both looked at each other and laughed. We thought we were laughing at the picture but I guess we were really laughing at each other. A guard walked by and smiled. "I'm glad to see you enjoying the painting," he said.

A similar painting was being auctioned recently and, when the auctioneer found it difficult to push the bidding over a thousand dollars, he turned the painting on its side and the bidding went up to two thousand. By then, people were getting into the spirit of appreciating modern art, and when the auctioneer turned the picture completely upside down, it brought over four thousand dollars. Everyone laughed, even the one who bought it.

For a long while I'd heard about the art show where the judge gave first prize to the air-conditioner panel in the wall, but I didn't really believe it until recently. I was asked to be one of the judges of a show of paintings from several of the most distinguished American prep schools. I couldn't come around to giving a prize to one painting that the other judges liked; it was just a framed field of solid blue. I like blue, but not that much. "You must admit," said one of the judges, "that it is a much more moving piece than the framed white-on-white next to it."

"Yes," I said. "I like it much more. But that 'white-on-white' happens to be the bulletin board."

Not all the jokesters of modern art are the painters. The critics are good, too. I saw one showing of completely blank canvases, done in various colors, and then read what a famous critic wrote, in a famous magazine: "These are pivotal works of the artist, for in the contest of Abstract-Expressionist noise and gesture, they suddenly brought one face-to-face with a numbing, devastating silence. Even granting the salvational overtones, an implication that no work was done, no expected artistry was demonstrated, left the viewer with himself and the void in front of him. His shadow moved across the blank screen and it mirrored the stammering images of his unwilling mind because 'nothing' was intolerable."

If he could say that about a blank canvas, think what he might say about a real picture. I think he should get the medal. A blank one, of course.

My favorite story is about the gallery that had an eight-foot square of white with a black dot in the middle. "Good God!" said one art collector. "What a powerful composition! Is it for sale?"

"Yes, indeed," replied the director. "It is two hundred thousand dollars."

"Send it to me at once!" said the collector. "I can't wait to get it in my gallery where I can drink it in. And if the artist ever does another, let me be the first to see it."

Well, the artist let it be known that creations like this could not be done in an instant—it took grief and living and hard work. But in a few years he returned with another painting. This time it was an eight-foot white square with *two* black dots in the middle. Of course the collector rushed over to see it and again he raved about the qualities of this new masterpiece. "Would you care to buy this one?" asked the director.

The collector thought it over very deeply. "No," he said. "I think it is a great piece, but I do like mine better. This one is a little too *busy*."

I'd like to say a kind word or two for the small-town library. I like to browse, and I usually find something more important than what I was looking for in the first place. I know of one fellow who went to a small-town library for a book and married the librarian. In big-city libraries you must know what you want, then mark it on a card with your name and other information, hand in the card, and wait for a lighted number to announce that your book has been found.

The first time I went to the New York Public Library was for some information about "a man-eating tree," which I had read about in a Hearst newspaper many years ago. Actually, I didn't believe there was such a thing, but when a writer makes mention of anything like that, he should know something about it. So up to the information desk I went, and asked, "What do you have about man-eating trees?" The man gulped and glanced beneath his desk where I guess he keeps some sort of self-protection, and then he waved for a guard. Well, he led me to a distant wing where I did find books with accounts of plants that ate flies, and of one plant that ate a frog, but there wasn't a single plant with an appetite for mankind. It took a whole day. When I got back to my village library, I thought the librarian might enjoy the story, but when I got halfway through, she stopped me.

"I've never seen such a story in a book," she said, "but I remember seeing it in an old newspaper. Wait a minute and I'll get it for you."

When I wrote *An Age of Barns,* I decided there must have been some early American "how to" books telling how to build barns. "Why not try the New York Public Library?" my wife asked. It was worth one more try, so off I went. This time I went to the rare-book department and, like an expert, rang the bell at the brass gates. "What do you want?" said a lady. "But wait a minute—what is that under your arm?"

"That," I said, "is a bunch of my own reference books."

"Oh," she said. "You must go down to the first floor and check them at once. Then I presume you have a pass for getting in here?" My expression showed that I didn't. "Then," she continued, "go to the other wing and get a pass for getting into the rare-book department."

Well, after a half hour or so, I returned and rang the little bell again. "Hello again," said the lady. "What do you want now?"

"I want a book," I announced, "about how to build an early American barn."

"By whom?" she asked.

"I haven't the slightest idea," I said.

"Well, if you don't know what book you want, how can I help you? All of our books here are listed by authors."

"I told my wife this would happen!" I said, gruffly and a bit too loud.

"Please speak quietly," she said, "and explain exactly what you want."

"Well," I said, "imagine that I am George Washington. It is 1776 and I want to build a barn, but don't know how. There must be some kind of book. That book is what I want." I guess my voice drifted too much, for the head librarian came over. "What does this man want?" he whispered.

"He says he is George Washington," said the assistant, "and he wants to build a barn."

"No," I insisted. "I am not George Washington and I really don't want to build a barn. I just want a book about old barns."

Without letting me inside, the librarian pardoned himself, pored over a reference file, and returned with a slip of paper. "Here," he said, "are two books that should be exactly what you want. Hand them in at the correct window and wait until the light lights up your number there. Good day to you."

I looked at the slip and he had written down the name of two books. One was *Our Vanishing Landscape* and the other was *American Barns and Covered Bridges* and they were both by Eric Sloane. "I told my wife this sort of thing would happen," I mumbled, as I headed toward the exit sign.

In the old days there were good old-fashioned paint colors like Slate Blue and Battleship Gray. You didn't need a chart when you went to the paint store. Nowadays, paints have fancy names and they change with ladies' fashions. You'd think there would be only one white, but you have a choice between "Snow," "Birch," "Eggshell," and "Sunshine." Some of the fancy colors have names that an old-timer would choose to whisper in polite society, like Maiden's Blush, Cheek Pink, and Nude.

This all started with some public-relations expert who was working on the Wilson presidential campaign. He got Mrs. Wilson to say that she liked pink, and so out came all sorts of women's wear in "Wilson Pink." Later, there was Harding Gray and Truman Blue, but they soon got tired of such well-known colors, so dark purple became "midnight" and cream became "café au lait" and pink became "shocking." Mrs. Roosevelt had a gown of "mint silver."

The trouble with changing names and changing colors is that by the time you've done half your living room and run out of paint, that color has been discontinued and is out of stock. Of course, this sort of thing keeps the paint companies running. And the aspirin companies, too. I knew of an interior decorator who started the idea of painting each wall a different color. Everyone thought he'd invented something special, but he'd really run out of paint that the companies kept discontinuing.

One time I found a use for a can of paint I'd saved for a year or two, named Taos Blue. I painted my motorboat with it, but there was only enough for one side, so I went back to the paint store for another can. You guessed it. "Good gosh," the salesman said, "this *is* an old color! We stopped selling this about two years ago. But we have something new called Taos Red. I recommend it highly." "All right," I said, "I'll take it." And that's how I became the only one on the lake who went north in a blue boat named "The Blue Streak" and returned south in a red boat named "The Red Flash." It amazed my friends and made life that much more interesting for a whole summer. But when I tried to sell the boat, it didn't help at all.

When I left art school, I tried my hand at painting murals in hotels and restaurants, and in those days when they needed a room "done plain," I'd have my helper do that job, too. It was remunerative but it left me with a lot of left-over paint which I put into a fifty-gallon drum. One day, I thought, there would be some use for whatever color it all turned out to be. But the same miserable color persisted, a sort of bilious purple. To this day, I find that the same thing happens; mix a lot of colors at random and you get a bilious purple. Anyway, for a laugh I put a label on my fifty-gallon drum saying "Elephant's Breath," and I told people that I'd invented a brand-new color.

Then one day a man came in and wanted me to paint his new restaurant and bar. "What a coincidence!" he said, as his eyes fell on my labeled paint drum. "The name of my place is going to be 'The Pink Elephant' and I've been looking all over for the right color. Use that there paint and you've got the job."

Well, I thought I'd struck it rich. Everything went well, too, until I ran out of of Elephant's Breath, with one wall left to go. I tried to buy the right colors and mix them together to match the old stuff, but nothing worked. Someone suggested I just go to the paint store and just buy paint at random and mix that up, but that sounded too silly. So when the owner came by, I told him there was too much of one color. A slightly different shade on one wall, I told him, would keep the room from being monotonous. "Monotony," I continued, "will drive people away. Perhaps I can keep the same theme but come up with a slightly different tone. Shall I try?"

"You're a genius!" he said. And I really was.

"Man and Wife."

Every now and then, you hear of someone wanting to give a gift but saying, "I just don't know what to give. He has everything." Or a man wondering what he might give his wife for a wedding anniversary. Well, one of my enjoyments in this life has been to revive some of the good customs of the past, and one of the very fine customs was that of giving "gift trees." I'll bet that will solve many of your gift problems. I hope so.

When newlyweds moved into a new house in the old days, friends came with fruit trees for the orchard and decorative trees for around the house. A husband would be certain to plant a fine "man-and-wife tree" in front of the house and at both sides of the front entrance. Many an ancient house has been properly dated by finding the age of these huge trees, and many a house has deteriorated or been destroyed, leaving only those trees as a symbol of what the house represented at one time—a home for a newly married couple.

Just after the Civil War, when iron was made with the heat of charcoal, many farmers sold their woodlots to charcoal dealers until the only farm trees left were the orchards and the two trees in front of the farmhouse. It is said that there were places in New England where you could climb a high hill and count the farmhouses by picking out these twin trees, the only trees left tall enough to be seen.

I have a friend in real estate who presents each customer with a tree for their new house. "I used to send them some champagne," he told me, "to toast their new home. But a tree lasts a long while and adds to the value of the property. Maybe I'll get to sell the same house again some day, and that tree I gave will help to sell it."

Each year, I present my wife with a gift Christmas tree and, when the holidays are over, we plant it on the grounds. I always forget what my other gifts were, but those trees are an unending delight for the rest of my life and for those who follow. I will admit it was a dubious delight to see the Christmas tree I planted the first year I moved to the country: its towering height and gnarled trunk make me all too conscious of my own age.

In this day when we no longer build for future generations, and trees almost always outlive the houses that man builds, I'd like to revive the custom of planting meaningful trees. The tree was originally the emblem of America, long before the Stars and Stripes came into existence, for the wealth of the New World at that time was its wood. And every time you plant a tree in honor of someone or some occasion (instead of sending flowers or champagne or candy) you are adding something valuable to your country, and thereby being patriotic.

In colonial times, on a certain day called Rogation Sunday, it was the custom for children to plant trees along the boundaries of the farm. Each year, on that day, the whole family would walk the boundaries and inspect these trees. Of course the children did not realize it, but they were in that way becoming familiar with land they would someday inherit, and they would know the exact boundaries because they themselves had planted the "bounding trees." Even now, many of the old deeds tell how the land runs "from this tree to that tree" although the trees have long since been chopped down. The new boundaries are now an iron post or a cement block. But I guess the whole land and countryside have less lore and romance. And trees.

Here lies ye Remains
of
ROBERT CAPLE^s

Born on
Sept 1, 1761
Died on
Aug 29, 1791

Oops!

People often wonder what made some of the early workmanship have that strange and almost indescribable charm. Very often, it came from an intentional variation from the monotony of regularity and conformity. We usually describe a chair or a house that isn't entirely squared, or a tombstone that has unequal-sized letters, as being "quaint." Well, I have news for you: the designer wasn't trying to be quaint. He was exercising the same freedom of individual creation that a painter does when he improvises and paints a bit more or less than he actually sees. I have often been astounded at some of the early tombstones that are magnificently carved with breathtakingly beautiful lettering, only to find that, at the end of a line of words, there wasn't enough room for the last letter. Then, with a tiny caret, the letter was added—looking very much like a mistake. Or sometimes a fine piece of old workmanship will be signed and dated with letters and numbers of varying sizes and degrees of stability. Some say the makers were drunk, some say they just didn't care. I say they bordered on genius and knew the rare value of being different.

When you see one of those ancient floors made up of wide boards, you feel a sense of beauty that is hard to match. I know of people who had wide boards milled to order but, when they were laid, there was still something missing. I told them that they should have had the boards sawed irregularly, with one end narrower than the other. That is how the old floors were done.

I remember an old-timer who helped me build a house, and I wish I had copied down a lot of the things he said. He thought the way people used to think, and at the time I didn't understand, but now that I am wiser and older, I often hark back and remember how sensible old Bert was.

Once I called Bert down for putting up a door in the most unorthodox manner. Instead of constructing a doorframe and then making a door to fit it, he nailed a door in place and built the frame around it. You won't hear of anyone doing that nowadays, but you will know how hard it is to fit a door to a frame; it takes many times of putting up and taking down, planing and cutting. The old way of building a frame around a door eliminates all of that. "I never heard of anyone making a frame to fit a door," I said. "You don't paint a picture to fit a frame do you?" he replied. And that stopped me.

Another time, I found a room two inches wider on one side than it was on the other. "It's all wrong!" I roared. "How can you have a room not squared?" "Well, my left arm is a half-inch shorter than my right arm," Bert said, "but I work harder than most folks with equally lengthed arms."

And so, almost half-a-century later when I built a studio, I enjoyed building a frame around a door and leaving the framework of the building a couple of inches out of whack. My helper thought this was poor workmanship, but maybe my building will outlast the average "ranch house" dwelling.

If you don't believe it, just measure both ends of any ancient piece of wide flooring and you will be surprised to find as much as an inch or more difference.

"But you just don't do that sort of thing," my friends said. "You just don't order planks that haven't parallel sides."

Actually, the old-timers were saving lumber as well as getting a sense of pleasing design, because the tree trunk itself is narrower with height. But as Bert once told me when I asked him, "Why in the world would you do such a thing?"—the stumping reply was, "Why not?"

A judge, you know, must be fair. He must not be "pre-judging" or, in conventional language, "have prejudice." That's what I kept telling myself when a group of nice people asked me to be one of the judges in an art show recently. And then I was confronted with examples of sculpture. There was a thing made of welded automobile bumpers, and another had an old tire suspended from a bedpost and the whole thing balanced on a motor block. A mobile was made from old wire with various cast-off engine parts dangling from a center pedestal that had once been a railroad tie. What do you do in a case like that? It's like being a judge in an art show where suddenly you are confronted with your mother-in-law as one of the works of art.

Junk sculpture is so accepted nowadays that you can't ignore it even if you can't understand it. Every bank or great new building you go into has some sort of decorative thing with wires and dangling beams in the lobby, and every art magazine features these things as major contributions to American art.

I feel that junk art is great for the junkyards. If those sculptors worked in the junkyard (where they get their material) and just rearranged their junk into mobiles and stabiles and constructions and Pop sculpture, then perhaps they might bring humor and life to an otherwise dismal mess.

Junk and art, in my simple mind, are opposites. Whereas art can be defined as something that brings beauty and usefulness into life and makes the world a better and more meaningful place to live in, junk is that stuff that has been cast away from life as being without beauty or use. That sounds pretty opposite to me. And if junk art can be brought into the fashionable galleries, then it should also be logical that the fashionable galleries, along with their paintings, could have their showings in junkyards.

The wondrous part of modern art, to me, is what will be done with it all. If you hint to any critic or art expert that you consider art as "something to hang on a wall," you aren't worth even talking to. You are regarded as unfit and completely ignorant. Yet despite the new glass walls and disappearing wall space, when someone spends a fortune on a painting he usually tries to find a wall to put it on. Let us say that you live in a city dwelling, and a rich uncle gives you a Calder stabile as a gift. You either have to build a house around it or move to the country. The Whitney Museum features a fuzzy object called "Untitled Box #3" (wood, pins, rope and stuffed bird), as a major work of art. I know what to do with a Picasso, but what do you do with a fuzzy object? Don't tell me.

I have a friend who sent to a Pittsburgh factory for a steel beam, which he welded to a pedestal. He then sent it back to a Pittsburgh gallery as a work of art. I have another friend who asks me to save all my old beer cans; he's making a "mobile construction" for his next showing in a New York gallery. I have a friend who melts old bottles and sells them as "glass collages." You may think I have strange friends, but I assure you they are all nice people and just as respectable as the people who buy their works. One neighbor has some gigantic steel stabiles decorating his lawn. "Don't they rust?" I asked him. "And why do you put them out in the weather?"

"I have to put them there," he said. "There isn't enough room for them in the house."

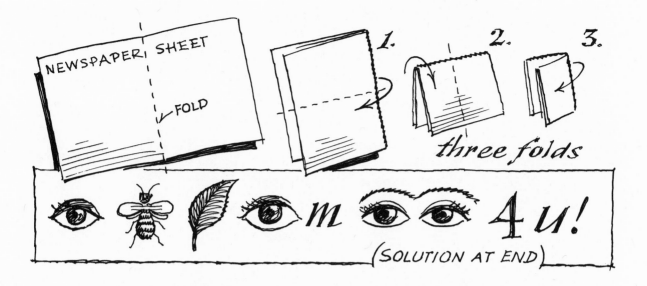

three folds

(SOLUTION AT END)

I've always insisted that a good painting "paints itself," and now I find that a newspaper column can write itself, too. What I mean is that a columnist gets a lot of outside help. Hardly a day passes without someone sending in a joke or a puzzle or something entirely usable. Just to show you what I mean, I'll devote this column to bits that people sent in to me last week. Ready?

Did you know that it is impossible to fold a piece of paper ten times? This means a *complete* fold (as shown above) and not just one small part of the paper. I tried it with a gigantic sheet of very thin pliofilm. Nine times was the limit. I guess you could win a bet on this one. Try it.

Then someone sent in the following wording, asking me if I could add the proper pronunciation marks so it would make sense: (solution at end)

THAT THAT IS IS THAT THAT IS NOT IS NOT IS NOT THAT IT IT IS

Then someone sent me a few unusual tongue-twisters. For example, try saying three times (or even twice), "TOY BOAT." You'd think that one is easy.

And someone sent in the following "latin" to be deciphered: Seville sedem go. Tousan busses inaro! Neville, demar trux. Vatsinum? Cowsandux! (solution at end)

I'd heard this one before but it's worth a mention: Tell me a simple four-letter word (a true word, not like "eenie, meenie") ending in ENY. The "eenie, meenie" throws you off, but try this on someone and see. (solution at end)

Best of all in my opinion, are the rebus puzzles. You know—like the old "ABCD goldfish. LMNO goldfish!" I guess the first rebus I learned was (solution at end):

YYUR, YYUB;
ICURYY 4 me!

But a century or two ago, when there were no radios or TV sets to take up

all the evening hours, they made up rebus puzzles that were whoppers. Here's
an example—solve the following address on a letter (solution at end):

WOOD
— — —
JOHN
— — —
MASS

And while we are hot on "over" and "under" puzzles, try the following,
which is a letter from one politician to another (solution at end):

STAND	TAKE	TO	TAKINGS
— — —	— — —	— —	— — —
I	U	THROW	MY

And up in New Hampshire there is an ancient rebus over a fireplace that is
still famous for being about the hardest one of all. Just to help you with it, I
shall give you the hint that the words "grate" and "fender" (for the fireplace)
are involved. And then, to help you further, you must know that in the early
days they didn't say "capital A" or "capital B" for large letters; instead they said
"great A" and "great B." You should also know that punctuations have names,
and the early American name for a period was a "full stop." Now I've just
about gone and given away the whole puzzle. But try it anyway.

If the B mt put:
If the B. putting:
Don't put : over a -der
You'd be an * it.

SOLUTIONS: 1. The drawing says: I believe I am too wise for you.
2. The punctuation added makes the sentence: That that is, is. That that
is not, is not. Is not that it? It is.
3. The Latin turns out to be: Say Villie, see dem go. Thousand Buses
in a row! No Villie, dem are trucks. What's in 'em? Cows and ducks.
4. My first rebus was:

Too wise you are, too wise you be;
I see you are too wise for me!

5. The four letter word is "deny."
6. The address on the letter is John Underwood, Andover, Mass.
7. The politician's letter said:
I understand you undertake to overthrow my undertakings.
8. The mantle rebus says:

If the grate be empty, put coal on;
If the grate be full, stop putting coal on.
Don't put coal on over a high fender;
You'd be an ass to risk it.

[38]

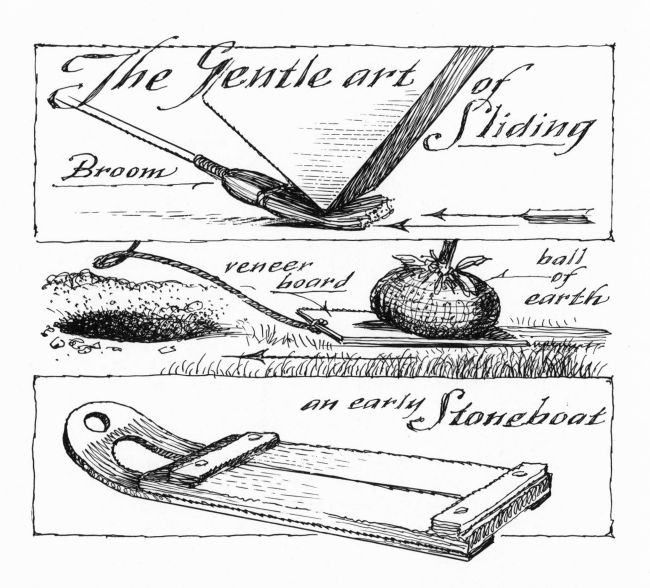

After you've written over a dozen books you will find that you soon begin to quote yourself. Then, before long, you will use yourself as an authority. My wife says she doesn't know what I'd do without my own books because every time she asks me a question I run to the bookshelf for them, to prove a point. Ruth recently sent a birthday cake through the mail, icing and all, but first she packed the box with a lot of popped popcorn. "It protects the cake nicely," she said, "and besides, you can eat the popcorn packing with the cake's sweetening on it."

"Where on earth did you ever hear of that?" I asked.

"Read it in one of your books," she replied. "There's a lot of good stuff in them if you're willing to wade through the rhetoric."

Last week I was dismayed with the task of moving an electric refrigerator into a guest house, and Ruth came up with a solution. "Just balance it on the end of this broom," she said, "and I think we can slide it in easily." It slid over the lawn, across some mud, up the step and right into place in the kitchen.

"Don't put that one in a book," Ruth commented. "You'd be repeating yourself. You should try out some of those early American things you write about. I've been sliding furniture that way for years. It keeps it from scratching the floor."

Actually, the idea of sliding things was an early American art. All those gigantic stones you see in foundations and those doorstop slabs weighing a ton or so were held in waiting for the winter sliding season and moved with ease on "stoneboats." Even in summertime, you could slide a stoneboat over long grass much more easily than you could pull the same load on wagon wheels. Wheels sink into the earth but runners slide easily. If a farmer had two wagons, he most likely had six sleds or sliding vehicles for heavier loads. I remembered this when I tried to wheelbarrow a load of firewood across a muddy lawn. But I didn't have a stoneboat or a sled. Ruth was watching me from a window. "I think I'll go look for some sort of sled," I said, and left the scene.

I looked throughout the barn but there wasn't anything there like a stoneboat. When I returned, the load of wood was gone. Ruth had found an old corrugated pasteboard carton and had tied a rope to it; then, piling the wood into the carton, she found it slid across the lawn with little effort. "You think you're smart, don't you?" I said. "Not necessarily," she replied. "I just read good books."

If you've ever tried to plant a live tree with the ball of earth on it, you'll know what a dead weight is. Most people lift it if they can, and wheel it to where it is to be planted, but that's doing it the hard way. If you just "sidle" it onto a flat piece of veneer board that has a rope attached to it, you'll find there is no lifting at all, and sliding is simpler than wheeling.

Somehow or other, the idea of sledding sounds primitive and slow. But iceboats have been clocked at over a hundred miles an hour. And when they wanted to test a rocket motor for really high speed, they put it on a sled. With an air cushion to take away some of the weight, according to scientists, the vehicle of tomorrow is going to be a flat-bottomed sled.

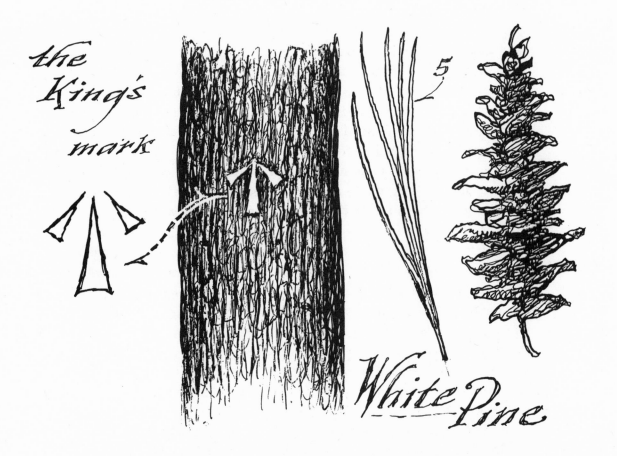

the King's mark

White Pine

Books have been written about the early American white pine tree; how the British sent experts over here to mark our best pines with the King's Broad Arrow so that they might be reserved for masts in His Majesty's Navy. Every now and then you will hear of pines that still bear that ancient mark. I have mentioned this tale in my writings, and, indeed, one day I searched a pine grove for the King's Broad Arrow. Some of the pines were as straight as billiard cues, with their lowest branches over seventy-five feet from the ground.

As I leaned against one of the giants, sighting with admiration along its straight surface, an old man walked along the road and greeted me. "Sure is a big 'un, isn't she?" he said by way of a hello. He was a very old man, so stooped that he had to cock his head to one side as he looked up when he spoke. "You looking for anything special?"

"I'm looking for a pine with the old British arrow mark. They saved these pines for masts, you know."

"Oh yes," he said. "I've heard about that. But I know my trees, lad, and there's one tree that is soft and splintery and not worth a goddam for mast wood. That's the white pine. Anyone knows that."

And there in the Cathedral of Pines that morning an American legend was shattered. The old man was completely right.

It took a bit of researching, but I think I found the answer. In several early manuscripts I found the Europeans and English referring to all evergreen trees as "pines." So remember you heard it here, folks—the King's Broad Arrow went more often on spruce trees than on the great American white pine. Furthermore, the great warships of early days did not use single tree lengths for each section of mast; instead, they used the heartwood of several trees laminated together and bound by iron hoops. I believe our "Constitution" had a lower mainmast with four such iron-bound heartwood sections that held together in spite of being hit by cannon shot. So my ideas of tall pine trunks being made into masts for the King's Navy has been much revised.

But after taking away some of the credit from this tree, I'd like to add that the white pine should still take a bow for being America's most famous tree. In fact, when the colonies decided to design themselves a flag without the British influence, they chose a flag with a white pine on it. The same is true of our first coins: the Massachusetts Bay Colony's Pine Tree shilling. The white pine was at one time this country's major national asset. Indeed, it is a mystery that its significance has so completely disappeared or where the eagle and stars and other unexplainable American symbols came from. Perhaps some day the white pine might appear again on a national seal or on our currency. Or even a postage stamp.

Few of us have thought about it, but pine is still the all-American lumber. Any good builder will tell you that such softwood is not proper for house framing, yet this is almost the only framing wood you can find in the American lumberyard. Pine is so plentiful, fast-growing, easy to cut, and good to look at that no other lumber sells as well. And pine is still the American asset it always was, being the prime source of paints, tars, turpentine, a thousand medicines, and many industrial chemicals. Even the paper these words are printed upon probably began in a pine grove.

Halo before Rain

Fuzzy moon, Rain soon.

Sharp Horns) sign of wind

Full moon for frost

THE THOMSONIAN BOTANIC

ALMANAC,

FOR

1839:

BEING THE THIRD AFTER BISSEXTILE, OR LEAP YEAR, AND
OF AMERICAN INDEPENDENCE, SIXTY-FOURTH.

Calculated for the Meridian of New Haven, but will answer for
any of the adjacent States.

CONTAINING

Extracts from the writings of the most eminent Phy-
sicians, in proof of the absurdities of *their* practice;
and some extracts and interesting matter in
favor of the *Botanic Practice*, and its
superiority over the *Mineral*.

NEW HAVEN:

PUBLISHED BY E. METCALF,

AND FOR SALE BY THE THOMSONIANS, AND MOST BOOK-
SELLERS THROUGHOUT NEW ENGLAND AND NEW YORK.

HITCHCOCK & STAFFORD, PRINTERS.

The most positive weather folklore is still centered around the appearance of
the moon. And since the moon is still the clock that regulates our time and
calendar, it is easy to see why the old-timers regarded their moon-lore as
science instead of superstition. Furthermore, as the moon is involved with the
mechanics of tides and frosts and water levels, it seems logical that the moon
might also affect the water or moisture in all living things, even human beings.

Benjamin Franklin's scientific theories were remarkably sound, and at the
time of his death, he was encouraging his friends to keep records of moon-
phases in regard to their personal and farm activities, in preparation for a study
of moon effects.

In my quest for collecting information from old almanacks, I recently found
myself fingering an original Benjamin Franklin edition, the kind that had an
extra blank page for each month. It seems that Ben sent these to special friends
at Christmastime, and the blank pages were for their personal diary notes.
This particular copy was sent to one of his neighbors, named Isaac Norris,
the fellow who sent the order to England for the first Liberty Bell. And Norris,
on one page, had penned in flowing script, "Put in my root crops during the
waning moon."

If you asked anyone nowadays what a waning moon is, not many would know what you are talking about. In this time of lunar exploration it is remarkable how much we leave to the experts and how little the average man knows for himself. In Franklin's time, even a child knew all the general facts about the moon. Now we talk about a "new moon" without knowing that a true new moon is entirely without light; we talk about a "half moon" without realizing it is really either a first or third quarter. There are some who aren't even aware that the moon moves overhead in the same direction as the sun. And it was the old almanack that children used for a calendar which taught them so many of the things they were expert at, and of which we are so generally ignorant. When it is the right time for curling up with a good book, I often choose one of my antique almanacks and find them most worthwhile.

Recently when my wife was ailing and all the local doctors seemed to be away on vacation, I put my tongue in my cheek and looked up her symptoms in my ancient medical almanacks while waiting for one doctor to call back. The symptoms, according to *The Thomsonian Almanack of 1839,* indicated "either chilblains or scarlet fever," and offered several remedies of hot teas made with herbs. Later, when the doctor arrived, he did a lot of humphing and silent nodding to indicate professional uncertainty. "It looks to me," he finally said, "like either chilblains or scarlet fever. Let's start by giving her some hot tea with medication."

Another time I wakened to find I had lost my voice with a sore throat. An almanack told me how George Washington died of quinsy sore throat, and my own symptoms seemed quite the same. Besides bleeding (which really killed the poor fellow), the other cure was "rolling a horn of paper with baking soda in it, aiming the small end at the sore spot in the throat, and getting someone to blow into the large end of the cone," which I decided to try.

I guess I put too much baking soda into my cone of paper, and I should have first explained the procedure to my wife. I just called her into my room and said, "Ruth, do me a favor. I want you to blow into this thing." Well, I guess she thought it was some sort of contest, for she put her whole self into the game. When I came to a few seconds later, she asked, "What was that white stuff that came out of your ears and your nose? And why did you want me to blow into the paper?"

"It was to help my sore throat, you nut! It was to give me back my voice!" I roared.

"Well you certainly have your voice back," she said.

I still pore over the old almanacks and there isn't one that doesn't provide a bit of useful information. Which is more than I can say for the novels some people curl up with.

Bells are for ringing!

Every year along about when the snow is heaviest, my wife sweeps out her "bell studio" and starts to work. Since we supported the revival of the early American custom of ringing bells on Independence Day, Ruth decided the project of annual reminders is her responsibility. So in mid-winter she begins typing letters to Governors and broadcasting stations and organizations and churches and whoever might keep the bells ringing.

When the replies begin coming in, the bell studio overflows with letters. "Don't walk on that pile," Ruth will say. "You're on the Wisconsin Governor's correspondence. Step over there on the Ohio Boy Scouts but take your shoes off first." Some of the letters are worth framing. One was from a Detective and Protective Agency who offered to let all their burglar alarms go off. Another told of a minister who set the electric church bell to ring at two o'clock the next day (July 4) before he left for his vacation. So, because only he knew the combination, the town "had Independence Day every day for a whole month."

One lady didn't like the idea. She didn't write—she telephoned. "I'm calling from New Rochelle," she said, "and I heard you on the radio. What are you—some kind of a nut? This idea of ringing bells on July 4 is complete madness! Haven't you heard of the anti-noise campaign in New York? Think of all the little children who are taking naps. Why, I've already gathered a group of mothers here in New Rochelle to stop your goddam bell-ringing campaign. If you must be 'patriotic' why not become a male nurse and be a boon to mankind? You must be some kind of nut!"

I tried to explain that it wasn't my idea at all—it was started by a guy named John Adams when he wrote to his wife, Abigail. But I didn't get very far, and indeed I did think about becoming a male nurse.

One letter was from a stern Britisher who insisted that ringing bells was an affront to Great Britain, and that the whole thing might start the war all over again. Another letter actually told of a British-born minister who closed his church and locked the belfry on Independence Day.

Another letter was from a small town that thought the idea was great. They formed an organization with a director and aides to publicize and direct the bellringing, and then they found there wasn't a single bell in town.

In one of my first weekly newsletters to the newspapers of the country, I said that "bells would ring everywhere, from radios in airplanes to the depths of the deepest mineshafts." It sounded dramatic but Ruth didn't like it. "There you do again with your rhetoric. *What* bells in *what* mineshaft?" But the next batch of mail had a letter from the Morton Salt Company's president: he said he was arranging for his salt mines (which work even on that day) to broadcast bell ringing at two P.M. (EDT). So there are a few laughs in it, too. It's worth all of Ruth's work, as well as the unmade beds, the dishes in the sink, and the burned toast in the morning.

There usually comes a time in a fellow's life—if he lives that long—when he decides he'd like to leave something behind when he goes. Having been a spendthrift, I've learned that leaving money behind is a poor and empty choice. And not having a cent of life insurance, I depend on my printed words to keep on working for a long while. But what I really mean is that a lot of us in old age get religious and believe we should leave the world a better place.

And so one day I too got to thinking how my books will eventually reach the remainder list and my paintings go out of style. And the thought of the whole country ringing bells on its birthday every year, and knowing I had a part in it, is a satisfaction. People will forget who dreamed up the idea of reviving that early American custom, but perhaps they won't forget to keep America's birthday a meaningful day.

the Trials of Art

Every now and then, someone telephones me asking if I give lessons in painting. Of course, I don't. But if I did, the course would be divided into two parts and the first part would be devoted to just plain chatting. I'd tell about all the trials of being a painter, how the rest of the world becomes something to contend with, what price to ask for your work, where to exhibit, and how to reply to stupid questions. These items are of major importance to an artist, often more important than perspective and shadow. They are things you have to be prepared for if you want to be successful while you are alive.

When a painter leaves his studio door open, he must be prepared for people looking over his shoulder while he works. Once, when I thought I was alone during a particularly tedious painting session, I turned and found an audience of five people. "Where did you come from?" I asked. "Ohio," one of them replied.

"Now you take me," said one of them, although I had no intention whatsoever of taking him, "I just can't draw a straight line." This is a favorite statement of watchers. They feel compelled to tell any painter of their strange inability to draw a straight line. Yet there seems to be so little need in today's world for people who can draw straight lines. I really don't know why it should worry them.

"Actually," I confessed, "I can't draw a straight line either. That's why I use a ruler."

This usually stops disappointed line-makers in their tracks, but sometimes they go right on. "I see your point," they will say, "but what I mean is I just don't have the talent. But you should see my nephew. He draws likenesses. Give him a pencil and a pad and quick as a wink you have a picture. Tell you what—I'll bring him over some time and maybe you can give him a few pointers."

Then there are those who want to show you their work. They "just happen to have some of it with them," and it is packed into the luggage compartment of their car. They have the first drawings they made, all the things they drew in art school, and "some they did on their own." Actually, they were pretty awful, but after carrying them around for twenty years to show to people, they fall in love with them. So in my "chatting classes" I'd be sure to ask my students to paint fast and immediately throw everything away that they did. Never keep a portfolio of stale work that you can fall in love with. One of the tricks of good painters is to try and forget a painting the moment it is finished; that keeps your work fresh.

When you "take up art," you'll find a lot of people who are willing to help you along. They want to give you practice in making posters for the local church rally or the garden-club show. Nobody else seems to have any cardboard or poster paints. "When the garden club calls upon you to make posters," I would tell my class, "tell them this is your afternoon to do some gardening, maybe like mowing the lawn. So if one of the ladies will do your gardening, you'll do the posters."

I'll explain that every time there is an auction or a raffle for charity, someone will call upon the painter for a painting. "Tell them you'll give a hundred dollars," I will tell my class. "But the voice at the other end will always be shocked. 'Bless your soul,' it will say, 'we don't want money from you—just some little old picture you have lying around.' That's when to tell them you have more little old money lying around than little old pictures."

Maybe my class won't turn out to be the best painters of their time, but they will be darned successful.

A disturbing thing happened to me the other day when I tried to trace down the origin of the dollar sign. I can understand the cent symbol of a C with a stroke through it, but why the S with two strokes? The books gave vague explanations: all were guesses like, "perhaps Doric columns through the letter S for silver." What disturbed me was that most explanations added that "the dollar sign might be the letter U over the letter S (for U.S.)." Why should that disturb me? Simply because the symbol for money and the symbol for my country might be the same thing.

A name or a symbol can be a most important thing, particularly when you are trying to sell an idea. Communism, it seems, has a pretty good symbol; a hammer for labor and a sickle for agriculture are symbols of a high and worthy basis for civilization. But the dollar sign is a tough emblem to sell the world on—it's what makes us the ugly American to many of the poor nations. If you don't think so, imagine yourself a cartoonist who has been given the job, first, of portraying a worker (or agriculturist), and then of portraying a banker. You'd begin with the banker by sketching in the inevitable bag of money. Already you've made him objectionable. Yet it is difficult to caricature a farmer or worker without making him seem a pretty good fellow.

Well, there's nothing we can do now about that dollar sign. We're stuck with it. But we can still do something about the word "capitalism" which is one of the ugliest words in the international language of thought. In the first place, although the word may mean one thing to us and sound very fine, to a non-English-speaking European, capitalism logically means "the worship of money." It is all right for us to explain that we don't really worship money and that the title is actually misleading, but why, then, do we use it? "Capital" in the dictionary means "money," and "ism" means "religion or doctrine; often applied satirically or with derogatory force." Put them together and the result is the way others see us.

I tried to disprove this to a Chinese student once, and he took me to my own dictionary (not new, but still titled *Practical Standard Dictionary of the English Language,* New York, 1929). He pointed to the following entry. "Capitalism: 1. A system that favors the concentration of capital in the hands of a few. 2. The power and influence of concentrated capital." Even an American wouldn't buy that sort of thing; it is worthy of the greatest contempt. Still, we are trying to sell ourselves (under the banner of capitalism) to the rest of the world.

So I am all for burying this ugly word which isn't in the Declaration of Independence or the Bill of Rights or any of our original thinking, and for letting people know we don't worship money. Let them know we have such contempt for the stuff that we enslave it and make it work for us. I'll bet Madison Avenue could come up with a good campaign along those lines, and what we need more than anything else nowadays is some good international advertising.

Witchcraft
---Twentieth century

Sooner or later, all homespun columnists get around to doing a piece about dowsing and divining rods. So, while my sleeve-garters and eyeshades are still new and the big syndicates haven't yet recognized me as the hottest thing since Walter Winchell, I want to get my water-witching story over with. To begin with, I don't believe a word of this folklore, but if you believe in it, God bless you.

I have a friend who swears his divining rod finds water anywhere and he carries it with him in his attaché case when he goes to work. Sometimes he tucks it under his arm and then waits for comments. He meets a lot of people that way and, as he happens to be an insurance agent, I guess his divining rod gets him business. When he reaches his office building, he will walk down the hall holding his water-witching stick properly until he reaches the men's room; then things begin to happen. The stick quivers and quakes and he can hardly hold it from pulling him right through the door. He swears he can find the washroom in any building this way. At least it entertains whoever might be going by.

In the beginning, when the hazel tree was supposed to be a bewitched plant (because it has a strange "wet" odor, and because it blooms when other trees have lost their leaves), people made hazel "witch sticks" for fun. These were just "magic sticks" supposed to do all sorts of miracles. A forked willow stick was supposed to find hidden treasure, and finally it became the implement for "finding water."

Nowadays, of course, they use any kind of a branch. If you want to find hidden coins, you make a slit in your divining rod and insert a coin. Look for hidden pipe by holding a piece of pipe in one hand, along with the rod. And you thought witchcraft was dead?

A while back, at the height of the drought, I decided to dig a well on my hilltop, and the cost was estimated at over two thousand dollars. "But I recall an article in an old *Popular Science*," I told the well digger, "about a 'point well.' They are supposed to cost less. Do you know about them?"

"Oh yes," he said. "They only cost about twenty dollars. But it might not work." That seemed quite a difference, and twenty dollars isn't so much of a gamble, so I ordered a point well. The man came around the next day carrying only a pipe with a point on the end of it. Then he hammered it about fifteen feet into the ground and screwed a little old fashioned hand pump on the upper end and when he pumped up and down, water came out. "Well, I'll be damned," he said.

I'll bet if I had used a divining rod, that story would reach the front page of *The New York Times*. "What do you think of water-witching rods?" I asked him. "Oh I think they're great," he said. "People who use them usually don't reach water, so that gets me an extra job of digging a little way over this way or that. A funny thing though, they still get the diviner to find the second or third place, and then give him credit if there is water there."

Now don't think I'm against superstition, because superstition can often take the place of confidence. It can make you a better guesser. Like the case of the prince who wanted to kill the dragon. He went to a witch and asked if she could make him a magic sword. "I just happen to have a magic sword on hand, very cheap," she told him. "Of course, you have to fight just as hard with it, but you are guaranteed to win every fight."

Well, the fight was a tough one, but the prince did kill the dragon. "The sword did the trick," the prince told the witch. "No," she replied. "That sword wasn't magic at all. It was just an old sword I had laying around. But it gave you confidence and confidence fought your battle for you."

I think the divining rod gives you the confidence to be a pretty good guesser. But stop making that rod quiver, fellow. You're killing me!

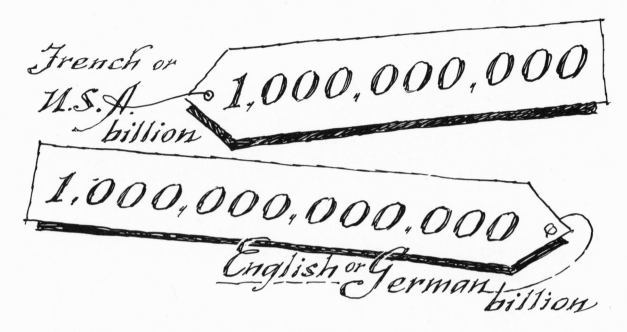

My *Webster's Dictionary,* in discussing numeration, says: "It seems that billions and higher denominations were never anything but a fancy of arithmetical writers. The probability of this is increased by their meaning different things in different countries." I just read in today's paper that New York State is asking for a tax amounting to "a fancy of arithmetical writers" (two of them), for working on water pollution. I guess finance is getting fancier and fancier.

A Congressman will think nothing of asking a billion-dollar appropriation without even knowing what a billion is. So you think he *does* know what a billion is? Well I have some news for you—*nobody* can know or visualize exactly what a billion of anything is or even looks like. No wheel, to my knowledge, has ever turned a billion times, even those on that antique Model A that I keep going year after year. If you make ten trips to Miami from New York, you'll find you haven't yet covered a billion inches. Or take a fast military propeller plane; if it could go at top speed for a year (which of course would wear out a lot of engines) the propeller would not yet have turned over a billion times. Or try to stack a billion new dollar bills. Would they reach a ten-foot level, or maybe fifty feet? No; they would go sixty-seven miles up, into the stratosphere! All right, let's take measurements we are more familiar with—a wooden kitchen match. Let's lay a billion of them side by side (not end to end, mind you), and guess how many feet or miles they would reach to. Believe it or not, they would go from the east coast right over the prairies and cities and mountains and reach the west coast. You couldn't lay the matches end to end, not on this earth anyway. They would be over fourteen thousand miles longer than the earth's circumference.

A billion, as far as I am concerned, is something the brain just cannot visualize; it is an entirely incomprehensible word, except in mathematics. Even in mathematics it gets confused, because a billion (as used in the foregoing examples) is a thousand millions, but in England it is a million millions, which is quite a bit of difference. I often wondered if they borrow in English billions and pay back in American billions. Perhaps our loans get so confusing that we just forget the whole thing and make it a gift.

I suppose within another century the billion will be old hat and the trillion will be in the headlines. A trillion by the way, is a thousand billions (twelve zeros) but, if you are German or English, it is a million billions (eighteen zeros).

It is all very interesting, but what more can we do than just be amazed? Well, I have an idea I'd like to share with you. I'd like to introduce the idea of a museum of awareness or concept—a building where young and old could go and get an idea of what all the things we talk about so freely really look like. We know what a foot and an inch and a yard look like, but exactly how far away is a mile? I'd put a flag or a marker a mile away, and a half mile away, too, with a window in my museum saying "That marker is a mile away and that one is half a mile away." I'd lay out one acre on the lawn. I'd lay out a thousand things and a hundred thousand things and a million things. And try somehow to lay out a billion things. I'd make a model of the earth and the moon not as most museums make them but in true and proper proportions. Let's, for example, make the earth about the size of a basketball, so the moon would be about the size of a tennis ball; now, instead of putting them a foot or two apart, let's put them thirty feet apart. Then students would get a proper idea of the vastness of space. Perhaps then we might add the sun, which would be a globe about one hundred feet in diameter, situated over two miles away, viewable again, out of a window. A diagram of a meteorological warm front has always been shown incorrectly because it is limited to the size and proportion of a textbook: in my museum there would be a warm-front model one foot high and a hundred and fifty feet long. These models would be the only truly scale models in the world of such natural phenomena.

I think a lot of people would like my museum, but I'm sure the million and billion concept models would particularly interest Congressmen.

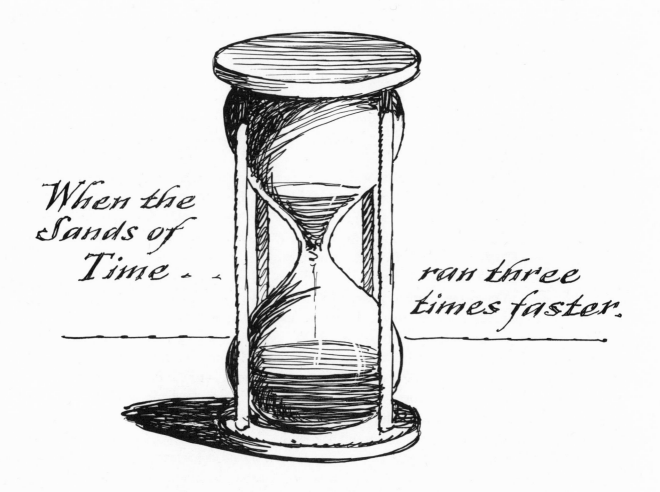

When the Sands of Time . . . ran three times faster.

The most common remark about the things created in the old days is, "Oh, those folks had all the time in the world." When we see the ancient houses with tremendous beams, built with infinite care, there is always the same weary comment, "They had the time."

That is a most thoughtless and completely untrue statement, for they had very little time. It is we who have "all the time in the world." To begin with, the average lifetime was once only about half of what it is now, so that cuts the percentage fifty percent right there. Also, the early days were much shorter because there were no lights sufficient for night work, or even for bad-weather days: rain or snow or cold often stopped work completely. Getting to work and home again by horse could cut your workday by as much as one half, but let's settle for ten percent less worktime. Now consider the time savers of today— the electric machines and tools. And then consider that before leaving for work, the old-timer did chores often equal to a whole day's work now. So, if you add this all up, you'll find that the old-timer did not have "all the time in the world," but he had, rather, about one third or less of the time we have now. He did, however, work harder.

I shall breathe a sigh of relief, and shake the hand of the first man who remarks, "How on earth did they do such good work with so very little time."

How they did so much in so little time makes interesting research, and I came up with one enlightening point that becomes more important the more you think about it: they went to bed earlier and arose earlier. One almanack gave me the lead, saying, "Mornings are like the youth of mankind; afternoons are like later life. Bedtime is no time for anything but reflection. Mornings are best for work."

They say that when a New England farmer gets a holiday, he gets up an hour earlier in order to get in a full day of loafing. Early morning, according to scientific research, is the best time of day for the human being—both mentally and physically. Not only is the body in its best condition (fewest deaths occur between six and seven in the morning), but the mind is most alert. If you want the answer to a perplexing problem, it is said, think about it before going to sleep and you will wake up with the answer.

In the early morning the world is undoubtedly at its best. The air is clearest, water cleanest, weather least violent, and the health of man and beast at their peak. So it seems that late sleepers are missing a lot out of life. Benjamin Franklin started that "early to bed, early to rise" jingle, but he little practiced what he preached. (Anyone who has read his early private diaries will be shocked to learn how very little.) In his youth, he worked far into the night and then slept till noon. But in one of his letters he wrote: ". . . still thinking it something extraordinary that the sun should rise so early, I looked into the almanack where I found it to be the hour for his rising on that day. I say it is impossible that any sensible people should have lived so long by the smoky, unwholesome, and enormously expensive light of candles, if they might have known that they had as much pure light of the sun for nothing." So Franklin discovered the sun, and wrote his "Early to bed and early to rise, makes a man healthy and wealthy and wise." And with only thirty percent of the time we now enjoy, Ben and the others of his time got a lot of work done—and done well.

the Dear old Past

When a fellow becomes known as an antiquarian, he gets into all sorts of trouble. In the first place, he feels like an antique. Then he gets on the list of "possible speakers" among the historical societies and, since saying "no" gets monotonous after a while, you have to say "yes" just to break the monotony. That's what happened when the King of Prussia Historical Society (Pennsylvania) asked me to speak.

"What can I talk about?" I asked the kindly voice from K. of P.

"Well, we thought you might give a talk on early outhouses. We've never had a talk on that subject."

I thought she was joking, but no. And that did it. There, to my mind, was a misled Society and one that needed a good talking to. So before I hardly knew it, I was on my way to the quaint town of King of Prussia.

Actually, there is a lot of outhouse lore, such as the crescent moon (Luna symbolized womankind) sawed into the door. The story is that originally there was also a nearby outhouse with a sun (Sol symbolized man) and these two symbols were just like our modern "Ladies" and "Gents" signs of today. But in the late 1800's when the country inns became less elegant, the men's outhouse was discontinued because of the proximity of the forests or bushes, and only the outhouse with the crescent remained.

But I concentrated on calling the society down for collecting useless information and things just because they are old. Some societies are the collectors of obsolescence and age instead of being museums of the past's good things. Children are impressed with old stuff like wooden washing machines and the ugliness of ponderous gadgets, but not favorably. They go away saying, "Oh, boy, I'm glad I didn't live then," and, to my mind, the historical society has then defeated its main purpose.

I told of a bewhiskered friend named Jon Pol who is in the business of collecting junk and selling objects d'art. He can produce a thousand chicken legs or a like number of turkey legs. And he knows someone will buy them. Maybe for backscratchers. I sent a friend of mine, who collects buttons to see Jon. "I'll bet he has more buttons than anyone you've ever seen." Sure enough, I was right.

"You wouldn't want them," said Jon. "I'm saving them. I'd have to get a hundred dollars for them and that's too much."

"I'll take them," said my friend.

Jon couldn't believe his ears. "You must need a lot of buttons in your household," he said. So my friend told Jon how people collect buttons as a hobby and how valuable a rare button can be.

Jon was impressed, and he saw how zippers have made buttons obsolete, and therefore valuable. He also reasoned that the zipper would become obsolete, too. So he has already started collecting zippers, and if you ever become a zipper collector, go to see Jon Pol. He has the biggest collection of them in the whole world.

But the best anecdote about Jon has become a stock antiquarian story. It was about a dealer who spotted an old pine sink in Jon's kitchen as a "sleeper." (A sleeper is something of more value than the seller realizes.) "I know you can't sell that old pine washstand," said the dealer, "but I'm looking for some good pine firewood. So for the firewood in it, I'll give you five dollars."

"Good!" said Jon, "but wait a week till I find another place to put the stuff I keep in it."

The dealer could hardly wait for the week to end, and he finally called for his "firewood washstand find."

"Here it is," said Jon. "I had a little extra time so I chopped it all up nice for you." The dealer never knew if the firewood really had been the washstand or not.

The Great Bathtub Hoax

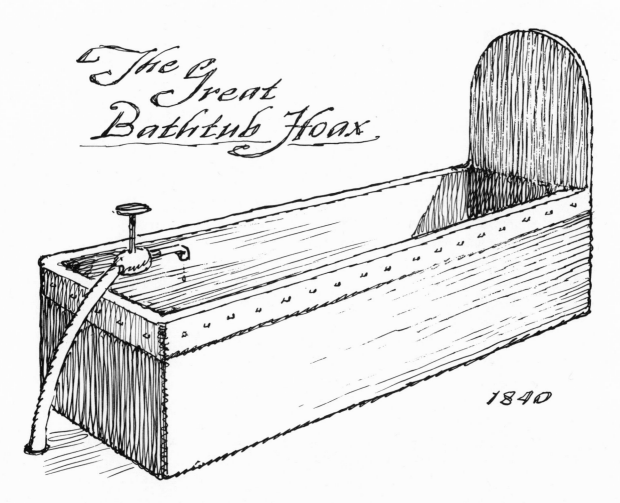

1840

Alas, I am a victim of allelomimetism. That is not a disease. It means that you've seriously copied someone who was only fooling. It seems that H. L. Mencken was once sitting around on a Sunday afternoon in Cincinnati, with nothing to do but to take a bath. So, while sitting in a tub of hot water, he dreamed up an imaginary story about the first bathtub in America. He gave names and dates and made his imaginary tub's weight 1,750 pounds. It sounded so authoritative that the story not only sold to the newspaper but reached the encyclopedias, and even appeared in dictionaries and news articles abroad. So when I wrote a child's book called the *A B C's of Early Americana,* and came to the letter B, I copied the false bathtub story from *Famous First Facts,* after researching it in several other books.

Since I learned of the hoax and how I'd fallen for it, I told my publishers about it, and asked to make a correction. But they insist their library agrees with the Mencken report. He certainly did a good job.

A lot of history has been written like that. Witness the Betsy Ross story. Her house in Philadelphia still stands, with a bronze plaque on it, but don't pin the historical society about her really having made the first American flag, for I'm sure they know different. Once I wrote a story about weather vanes, and told of the great sense of humor the old Maine fellows had. "We use an iron chain up here," said one of the jokesters, "and let it hang for a weather vane. When that chain stands straight out, we know the wind is ablowin.'" Would you believe it?—someone in writing a book about American weather vanes had taken me seriously and included the "Maine chain weather vane!"

Another time, I wrote a covered-bridge story in Old Sturbridge's magazine *New England Galaxy,* and when I told how the horses hoofs "clobbered through the portals of the old bridges," they misprinted the word as "cloobered." So far I've picked up three articles on how "the horses used to cloober through the old covered bridges." I suppose that word will turn up in a dictionary some day. This week I read how the city of Buffalo got its name from an Indian chief whose name wasn't buffalo but *meant* buffalo, which sounds pretty mixed-up. A little research, however, told me that the French, who first settled there, once called the place Beau Fleuve. I'll bet you a nickel that "Buffalo" is just a mispronunciation of that.

One place in Pennsylvania was called Bag O'Nails because that was the name of an inn there (according to legend). There really was no such inn, I learned, but there was an inn called the Bacchanalian, and you know darned well those Germans couldn't pronounce that one. It just must have come out "Bag of nails."

Then I'm told there's the place in New York State called Trumansburg that got its name from the Post Office Department. It seems they tried for a long while to get a post office in Triemansburg, but the application, which grouped the letters i and e together (looking like u) was accepted under the name of Trumansburg, so they just changed the name of the town.

The Post Office Department also named the town of Difficult, Tennessee, when they returned an application from the town of William's Crossroads. "The name of your town is difficult," said their letter. So, Difficult it became, and I guess if you look in your atlas you'll still find it under that name.

So be careful what you say: your words might go down in history. The fellow who first made up the name United States of America instead of "United States of North America" made the first boner in name-making, but it certainly wasn't the last.

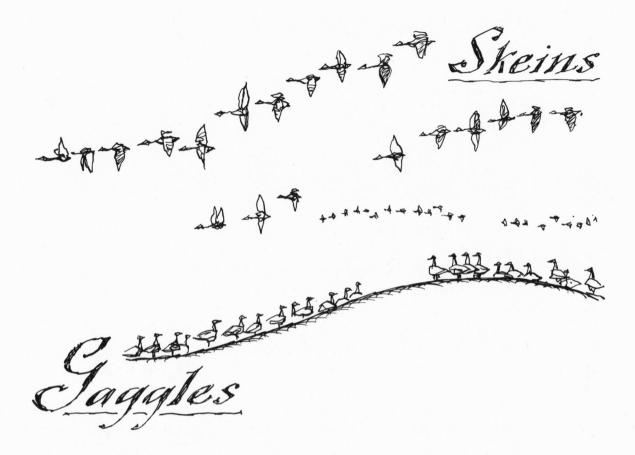

Skeins

Gaggles

In case you might want to know, the plural of mongoose is *mongooses* and not *mongeese*. Most people know the story of the zoo that ordered two of them without knowing, so simply made out the order for "one mongoose." Then, adding a postscript, they said, "On second thought, please double that order." Knowing that the plural of ox is oxen, you'd think that two musk ox should be "two musk oxen," but no, the language of animal assemblages is not that simple. Even the sportsmen have devised their own English, such as *hunting* animals but *shooting* birds.

While searching through early barn records I found the plans of a huge Vermont barn built "for two packs of horses." Having never heard of a "pack" of horses before, my research suddenly went into semantics, unearthing a goodly amount of names for birds and beasts in plural. Hunting-horses in the old days, it seems, were counted just like playing cards, in a "deck" or "pack" of fifty-two. So the aforementioned barn was designed for two packs, or one hundred and four animals. Perhaps you might be interested in some of the other names I eventually unearthed:

A *flight* of doves, an *exultation* of larks, a *sege* or *sedge* of herons, a *charm* of goldfinches, a *bevy* of quail, a *covert* of coot, a *herd* of swan, a *murmuration* of starlings, a *dopping* of shelduck, a *watch* of nightingales, a *fall* of woodcock, a *pack* of grouse, a *dule* of turkeys, a *paddling, leash, badeling* or *team* of duck, a *muster* of peacock, a *quarrel* of sparrows, a *skein* of geese (in flight), a *gaggle* of geese (on land), a *spring* of teal, a *wisp* or *walk* of snipe, a *nye* or *covy* of pheasants. And that about did it for the plural of these kinds of bird-life.

In the animal line, I found a *pride* of lions, a *lepe* of leopard, a *herd* of harts, a *bevy* of roes, a *sloth* of bears, a *gownder* of swine, a *route* of wolves, a *nest* of rabbits, a *down* of hares, a *skulk* of foxes, a *team* of oxen, a *stud* of mares, a *tribe* of goats, a *farrow* of pigs, a *flock* of sheep, a *harrass* of horses, a *rag* of colts, a *labor* of moles, a *clowder* of cats, a *shrewdness* of apes, a *richness* of martins, a *cete* of badgers, a *baren* of mules, a *drove* of kine. Of course "kine" is the plural of cow.

If you get a bunch of experts (oops—I should have said a *staff* of experts) together, you will find they use only the correct word. You will find they *kill* salmon instead of fishing for them or catching them; they *couch* a bear, *kennell* a fox, *watch* an otter, *bed* a roebuck, *harbor* a hart and *tree* a cat.

This collecting of early (and proper) plurals has become quite a hobby among the literate and sophisticated naturalists, and I recall a group of college boys walking down the street with their English professor. "What would you call those three girls walking ahead of us—that *covey* of quail or *batch* of tomatoes?" asked the professor to test his students' imagination and inventiveness. "Well," said one boy, "I might call them a *platter* or a *jam* of tarts." The next boy thought a bit. "You could call them a *novel* of Trollope's." It took a bit of digging for the next fellow who specialized in puns. "I'd call them a *troop* of horse." And then came the professor's turn; he topped them all with "An *anthology* of Prose, or possibly a *flourish* of strumpets or a *firm* of solicitors."

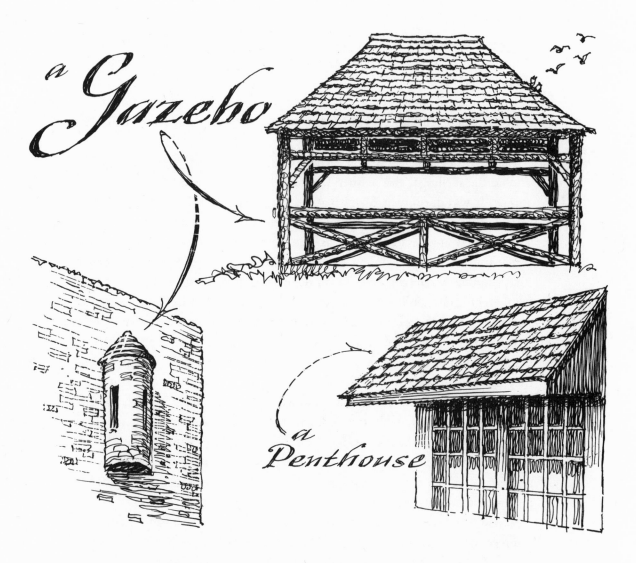

a Gazebo

a Penthouse

I like words. When they sound like what they mean. But when a word sounds like what it doesn't mean, I get mad. And, for spite, I just don't use it. Like the word "urban" which to me sounds woodsy and country-like and herby or "herban." Or take the word "penthouse" which we all use incorrectly anyway: if you look it up you'll find a true penthouse isn't a shelter or house at all—it is a narrow shed or roof or awning-like extension that projects outward over a window or door.

The other day during dinner my wife Ruth said, "Let's build a gazebo this summer," and I didn't know what she meant. But she and the others at the table agreed that anyone my age should certainly know what a gazebo is. A gazebo, they told me, is an open summer house. In fact, there was a play by that name which I guess was about a summer house. Well, I always called a summer house a summer house (which seems a fairly good idea), and when I was a youngster, everyone had one. They were cedar-posted open-sided houses on the lawn, and you had tea in them on summer days.

Also, when I was a lad, if a fellow was too smart for his britches, you called him a smart-alec or a gazebo. As the dictionary still puts it, a gazebo is a "shrewd fellow."

Even today, I often refer to some of my smart-alec friend as gazebos, and I always wondered why they looked at me so strangely. I guess they had never been called summer houses before.

Actually there are two words, each pronounced the same, *gazebo* and *gazabo* (notice the spelling), and neither one started out as a summer house, except by misuse. It was during the Spanish American War that soldiers used the word *gasapo* or Spanish for "durned fool" and that is how the name gazabo started. But I guess you have to be as old as I am to remember that kind of a gazabo.

Then, in the early 1900's, an English architect criticized American architecture, laughingly referring to the then popular summer house as "a silly piece of rural architecture, built like an open gazebo." Everyone in England knew that a gazebo (from the word "gaze") was a turret-like balcony on ancient castles which extended outward from the castle wall so you could spy on anyone climbing up. But the Americans never were good at the English language and they liked the sound of the word gazebo. So gazebo it has been ever since.

I still remember our old family summer house. It was big enough for two hammocks. Actually, both the summer house and the hammock are pure Americana. The hammock was invented by the Indians (woven from "hamac bark"). It was Columbus' sailors who first wrote about the strange "hamack beds in which the natives sleep." And the first hammocks made by the white men were made by the sailors themselves.

So, as an Americana buff, I think I shall indeed make a summer house this summer, with a good old-fashioned hammock in it. And when the weather is warm, if you stop by Weather Hill Farm, you will see a contented gazabo in his gazebo.

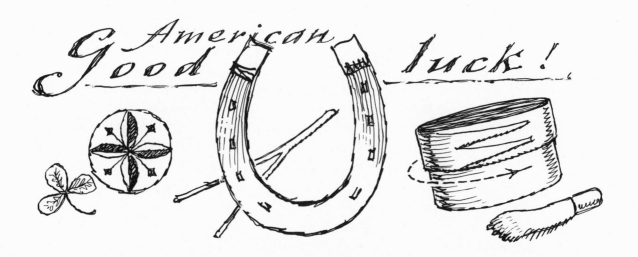

American Good luck!

Recently I did a column debunking the divining rod for "witching" water, and I got a lot of mail debunking you-know-who. "You're a fine antiquarian!" read one letter. "Contradicting good old American folklore! You should be just the one to collect and record such Americana." Another letter was from a pilot friend who offered a cash prize to anyone who will fly blindfolded with one of those witching sticks and tell when he is over the Hudson River. Another letter told how the New York City Water Department uses a chromium divining rod for finding water leaks. It was good fun reading, but it doesn't prove to me that there is anything in such superstition. It does prove that Americans have a good sense of humor. But fun is fun, and things can go a bit far, don't you think? Take the example of the big modern skyscrapers that refuse to have a thirteenth floor; you still find them because there are still people who won't rent a place on an "unlucky floor."

When I was a bachelor on the north shore of Long Island, I lived in a remodeled barn and it had a big hex sign on it, with the letter "H" in the middle. I painted it for fun, but it really did a good job of keeping jealous husbands away, and maybe even a few evil spirits.

One of my best friends still has the scar where a "lucky horseshoe"—that he hadn't nailed up too well—fell when he slammed the door. Few people know that our own George Washington started that horseshoe superstition. In a letter complaining about some soggy land that a neighbor was trying to sell him, he wrote that "If you ever lost a horse-shoe in such a mire, *you would be exceedingly lucky to ever find it again.*" Of course they leaned over backward to remember and revere everything the good General said, so for the next two centuries they regarded finding a horseshoe as a stroke of "exceeding good luck."

Another American folklore superstition is the one about the woodchuck, but it began in Europe where it was a bear instead of a woodchuck. There

[65]

weren't enough bears here, but there were plenty of woodchucks. The date of February used to be the day farmers made their spring planting plans: they went to church (Candlemas Day) and lit candles to pray for a good crop. All the interesting lore about the occasion, however, has been forgotten, and farmers don't pray for good crops anymore. But they do collect into groups that swear the groundhog legend is true. If you think I'm exaggerating, do you know that the Missouri Legislature passed February 2 as official Groundhog Day, and that a group who used February 14 instead of February 2 picketed in Washington to have the bill rescinded? It ended with Groundhog Clubs gathering into a national society with dues and meetings and all the window trimmings like buttons and cards and secret handshakes. It's too bad that when spring finally comes, the same fellows lose their reverence for woodchucks and work just as hard to make them extinct.

Very few folklore superstitions, it seems, are completely American. One is the belief that getting out of bed left-foot-first is bad luck: that stems from the early Shaker custom revering the word "right" (they bent on their right knee to pray, made their wooden box "fingers" bend to the right, and specialized in right angles). "Singing before breakfast being bad luck" also comes from the early American religious habit of morning rising prayers; the omen was originally, "singing before *morning prayers* is bad."

The daisy-petal ditty is also American, but at first it was not "He loves me, he loves me not, etc." It had other alternatives in the original ditty:

> He loves me, he don't; he'll have me, he won't.
> He would if he could, but he can't.

The button ditty "Rich man, poor man, beggar man, thief," is probably pure American because it ends up with "Indian Chief." The rabbit-foot superstition—supposedly Indian—is really a Negro superstition. Oddly enough, the American Indian was amazingly civilized for, with all his lore, he had more customs than superstitions. I cannot think of one American folk belief that I can trace back to our so-called "savages."

I think I'll take advantage of this age of revolt, when everyone can be fashionably against whatever he pleases without being condemned. Just for fun (and perhaps for some good too), this week I'd like to be against competition. Now in America to knock competition is like hanging the flag upside down or belittling motherhood, so I'm going to draw my shades after dark and not walk outside without my dog for protection. Although I admit the merits of competition, I think it's about time someone spoke up against making a national god of it. I think America is bigger than that.

To start with, I want to offer the thought that nothing really worthwhile in human behavior has ever been created by competition. As for better things and greater discoveries, it takes very little research to learn that no doctor ever found a cure for a disease because he was trying to outdo another doctor; no painter did better work because he was competing with another artist. The same thing goes for writers, scientists, educators, all along down the line to Christ, whose words will live forever—He wasn't trying to compete, either.

Great deeds, I think, are born from within and not from outside competition or a race to win.

America has done well with an economy built upon business competition, but to make this a religion or a way of life is downright immoral. Competition is fine if it results in better things, but competition all the way includes cheaper prices and cheaper quality too. It includes putting the little fellow out of business and it includes using money as a power to do just that. Competition at its extreme is evidenced in war.

I recall Japanese electric light bulbs that lasted only a few weeks, "made in USA" (USA was a town created just for that confusing title). I recall pencils that broke at once, and red erasers that made red smudges instead of erasing. I cursed the Japanese as creators of poor quality, instead of condemning the American distributors who certainly knew what they were buying and distributing. It was the American distributor who ordered "the cheapest price no matter what," and fooled the public, blaming the Japanese and using one of the major rules of competition to make the most profit. Now we have learned what the Japanese can really do, and of their reverence for excellence, even above their love of personal profit.

I recall when people walked or ran or swam or sailed for the pure sport of doing these things. Nowadays, sailing is no fun unless there is a race. The best American athlete is so often the one that brings in the biggest salary. Remember setting-up exercises? They went out of vogue because you weren't with anyone.

I recall when you could recognize the original Worcestershire Sauce by its one-and-only orange wrapper, when a Johnson outboard motor displayed a greater difference from an Evinrude than just color, when a Chevrolet could be more easily recognized from a Ford, and when a fellow could have his favorite bread or soap or breakfast food without a TV commercial entering his living room and arguing against it. Today there is a drab sameness about everything: many cigarettes taste alike, although Madison Avenue works hard to dispute it; all bread and cereals and radios and TV sets and gosh knows what are pretty much the same, with just a battle of prices that nevertheless still manage to keep rising.

Maybe competition will enter the field of individuality and excellence again. Till that time, let's not worship it blindly. Let's realize that America is not great just because of competition. Living and being of service to our fellow man isn't exactly like a football game or a heavyweight championship; it's a quiet process where we give something of ourselves instead of winning something away from the opposition.

Mr. Terwilliger

My favorite doorman, Mr. Terwilliger of New York's Biltmore Hotel, always looks forward to his annual trip to New England. "You're only old once," he says, "so you might as well make the most of it." Terwilliger has a lot of memories up in New England, and once a year he visits them.

All year Terwilliger breathes the city's exhaust fumes as each taxi pulls away from his door leaving a cloud of poisonous smoke. So his idea of a vacation isn't going to Miami. Instead, he goes northward and finds an old country road where he parks his car and takes a rake from the luggage compartment. Then he rakes a few leaves together and makes a small bonfire. He also carries a broom in case the sparks should go astray, and he carries a picnic luncheon. "It sounds pretty stupid, I guess, but it reminds me of my boyhood. And that," he says, "is worth the trip. It clears out the smell of city streets. Last year a fellow came by and wanted to know what I was doing, and I told him I just happened to like the smell of burning leaves, and he went away to get the sheriff."

I met Terwilliger on one of his annual jaunts to New England, when he showed up at my door with a big glass jug. "I see you have one of those old-fashioned wells," he said, "and I wonder if you'd mind my taking some of the water." That was about twenty years ago, but every time I drink my well water, I remember Terwilliger, and the water tastes better. In fact, it gave me the idea of keeping a good supply of my own tap water (which comes from the well) in the refrigerator of my studio. Then when people come by, I say, "How would you like some very special spring water?" It's a funny thing, but they act like they had never tasted the stuff before, and every now and then people come all the way from New York and bring their friends "to try Sloane's spring water."

On a hill near my place are the ruins of an ancient well from which water was shipped to the city. But now, in all the surrounding towns, when you turn the tap on you can smell the water across the room. Nobody rejects the chlorine cocktail when it arrives at the table, but let a Martini have the wrong brand gin in it or a Manhattan be a little too sweet and the bartender gets it back like a boomerang. Connoisseurs of cigarettes and liquor we are, but when it comes to drinking water, we're lunkheads.

I know of one place in Plymouth (Connecticut) where there is great well water, but it is rich with iron. The coffee you make with it comes out deep purple. So water is carried from another spring, just for coffee making. There're people who pride themselves on making "a good cup of coffee," without even a thought for the major ingredient, water. Some of the big-city restaurants have signs telling how their coffee is made from the best brand; I wonder if they will ever have signs telling how their coffee is made from pure imported spring water. Some day they will, for people will finally learn that their water is the filtered contents of toilet bowls which are emptied into the rivers where the drinking water comes from. Big-city water isn't as free as you might think. When taxes and piping and filtering and testing and other costs are considered, a glass of the stuff costs about what a glass of beer costs. It was Byron who reflected, "Till taught by pain, Men really know not what good water's worth."

So now and then when I get to New York, I fill a jug with just plain water and leave it off with Terwilliger. Have you ever noticed the joy in a man's face when you present him with a bottle of booze? Terwilliger's joy tops that.

Signs of the times.

The old-time inn signs featured remarkably good English as well as fine design. The word "hotel" was rare on the early signs (it wasn't even in the dictionaries) but "entertainment" was almost always the word used, and used correctly. Nowadays we use the word incorrectly, making entertainment sound like a floor-show instead of being no more than food and lodging for travelers. We "entertain friends for dinner" but when we look for entertainment in a public place we suddenly insist on some sort of theatrical performance or music.

Signs saying *café, package store, soda-pop, tonic,* and the like still tell you what part of the country you are in, but I guess New England has more hand-me-down language than any other part of the country. I have neighbors who shoot "mushrats", eat "sangwiches" and have "chimblies" on their houses. One local carpenter put a "cornish" on my house which he says makes it look "mid-Victorious." He knows a lady who raises "Rushing wolfhounds," and "nasty nurtions."

Somehow I wince every time I see those new highway signs that say GO SLOW. Why spend taxes to teach children proper English and then use improper English at home and on public signs? Some say we are just saving on letters or trying to make the sign easier to read, but then we could have just made it GO SLO. So I pray that some day the sign makers do right by their children and our language, and that when you approach an intersection, you will go SLOWLY.

Having started out as an itinerant sign painter, perhaps I notice signs more than the average person, and I find that signs are the art of current civilization as much as painting or sculpture. I get a bit bilious when I see signs that read EATS or DINER or QUICK LUNCH, some of which are bad English and some of which make no sense whatsoever. PIZZA PARLOR and PIZZERIA, HOT-DOG STAND, SNACKERIA and EATORAMA probably tell the story but they certainly don't spark the appetite. One imaginative horror is a roadstop with the sign EAT AND GAS UP. I belch at the thought of it.

About half a century ago, when I started out upon the world with my paint box and lettering brushes, I always had a handy supply of ready-made signs that I worked on at night in my hotel rooms. Justly ashamed to remember them, they nevertheless brought in a steady supply of money as I traveled on. One was always in "Old English" and supposed to appeal to the more sophisticated restaurateur: SERENELY FULL THE EPICURE MAY SAY. FATE CANNOT HARM ME—I HAVE DINED TODAY! Another was for the less sophisticated: I'LL CRANK THE CAR AND HOLD THE BABY, BUT I WON'T CASH CHECKS AND I DON'T MEAN MAYBE. What a fellow will do to make a living!

One of the inconveniences of being an itinerant sign painter is that you usually have to paint on a wooden board which first has to be given a couple of coats of paint, and that is time-consuming. The joy of the trade is when you can paint your sign and be on your way with the cash the same day. And so a school of old-time sign men developed known as "rock-men" who specialized in painting signs along the highways, on the flattish surfaces of rock: They had not the worry of constructing a signboard and waiting for the background to dry. The rock-men, however, had two identifying tendencies: one was for religion and the other was for strong drink. On their day off (I guess) or whenever they saw a particularly flat and prominent stone, they were compelled to make use of it. Therefore, you were often faced with glaring warnings of GOD IS RIGHT AROUND THE CORNER . . . or GOD IS LOVE . . . or PREPARE TO MEET THY GOD.

How sad that the lore of sign painting is gone, along with the reverence for fine lettering and good taste in signs. The conglomeration of road signs nowadays only adds to the ugliness and the tapestry of costly and well-made junk that is roadside America.

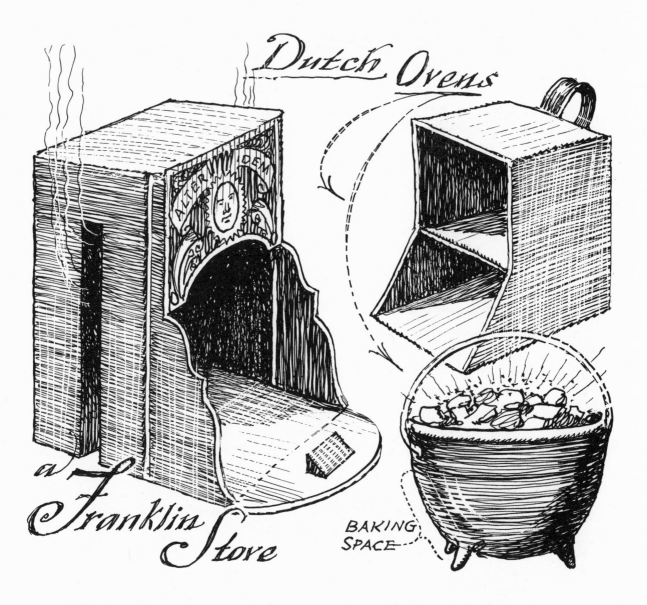

Dutch Ovens

a Franklin Stove

BAKING SPACE

Being known as an antiquarian and having remodeled a dozen early farm-houses, it still comes as a shock to realize that I have yet to see a real Dutch oven or a real Franklin stove. Of course, I've seen the so-called Franklin stove and even as I write these words, I sit alongside one of those squat, iron, open fireplaces on legs that manages to throw a bit more aesthetic warmth than it does actual heat. The gadget that Franklin invented was much more compli-cated: an eight-plate stove with a heat box inside that puffed hot air out its sides. It had a human-faced sun on the front plate titled "Alter Idem" or "an-other like me." It is said that Ben intended to market his invention under the name of The House Sun but he gave the idea away to a friend who had his own iron furnace. The friend, however, finally simplified the design into the present-day "Franklin Stove" which is nothing but an open iron fireplace made to fit into the wall instead of sitting out in the room the way we use it now.

[73]

The real Franklin stove is rarer than the Franklin almanack, and some day I hope to catch up with one.

I also hope to find a good Dutch oven—which isn't a wall oven at all—but an iron pot. There was also a tin screen fitted with shelves that baked by the reflected heat of the fireplace, and this was called a Dutch oven as well. But the first Dutch oven was a large iron pot with a concave lid that held hot coals as shown above.

So many of the words of our antique world are the result of more recent nomenclature, like the "old Kentucky rifle" which of course was made in Pennsylvania. Another example is the well known "grandfather's clock." When they were first made, they were known only as "coffin clocks" and not until a popular song came out in the 1800's about "grandfather's clock," did the new name take hold.

Being a word detective is fun, and my hobby of collecting old dictionaries has been a lot of help. I've come to the conclusion that the early American settler was, among other things, rich in his language. I don't mean English— I mean the American language, those words and phrases that were born here in Colonial days. Most of them have been twisted or lost completely, but you might be interested in some examples.

Today you will often hear the phrase, "stop fiddling around" and you im- mediately think of a fiddle. But in the earliest American dictionaries you will find the word *fettle* which meant "to do trifling business." "We are doing too much fettling," said John Hancock, annoyed at the time taken to compose the Declaration of Independence. So when you use the expression, make it "stop *fettling* around," and be correct.

Another early American word was *jackalent* which meant "a foolish fellow" or "a silly-looking being." So the "jack-o-lantern," which we thought came from the lantern made of a hollow pumpkin, really originated from the silly grinning face we cut into the pumpkin.

Nowadays the antiquarian will tell you that the main beam of a house, the one that carries the other floor-beams, is called a "summer-beam." Yet the correct word should be *sumpter-beam*. A *sumpter* was the strongest work- animal on the farm (usually a horse or an ox), and the *sumpter-beam* was the "work-horse beam" that did most of the work holding up the old-time houses.

It seems like only Yesterday!

I have a friend who just returned from a vacation, and I asked him what had most impressed him. "Well," he said, after some thought, "I guess the most impressive thing was the speed with which I reached Japan. Our lives are so short, that such a time saving is a major step forward in civilization."

"I suppose you're sorry to get back into harness," I said. "That long commuting trip back and forth must be a strain."

"Oh, I don't really mind it," he said.

It made me think. Here was a man who uses 1,450 hours a year just to go and come from work, day after day, the same weary grind without minding it. Yet he was impressed by the saving of a one day's trip by plane. I suppose I sound like Jules Verne, looking too far into the future, but I can foresee or hope for some method of getting to work in comfort. Perhaps even a diner on that wonderful vehicle, so I could eat breakfast on the way. I can see myself, being served poached eggs and bacon on a crisp white tablecloth, and reading the morning paper. But we had all this twenty years ago, didn't we? The railroad station that I used to embark from is now a gift shop and Army-Navy store. Once in a while a dirty train pulls through, with opaque window panes, with too much heat (or too little) and guaranteeing you the most miserable ride on earth. But if you want to go to Japan, that's something different. I often wonder if there isn't a lot of room for improvement at home and too much attention concentrated on competition to get to Japan or the moon. Of course, I could be wrong.

The other day I was trying to entertain some kiddies with imitations. After a cat meow and a cow moo, I tried out the old favorite of the train just making the hill and then racing down the other side. Then there is a long lonesome train whistle and a few toots at the crossing. I waited for some sort of applause. "What was that?" they asked. And then I realized that none of these youngsters had ever seen or heard a steam locomotive.

The Russians just announced their new railroad train will go a hundred and fifty miles an hour, with restaurants and the works. The stations, they say, will be as immaculate as their subway stations. That may spur us on, as we don't get inspired until someone else is in the limelight. I may sound unpatriotic, but I think it is somehow very costly for one man to walk in space comfortably for a few moments while the whole nation travels between home and work in slum vehicles.

Yesterday another railroad went out of business, and next to that headline the story about our billion-dollar research (that's just research alone) to design a plane that will get you where you want to go (if you happen to want to go in that direction) in about an hour less time. Actually, I never wanted to go anywhere that fast or at that price.

My boyhood memories are richer because of the steam train. Exciting as the modern airport terminals are, aviation has become poverty-stricken in lore. Planes travel over nations without your even being aware of where you are, but a train borrows from the land it goes through. If you should want to know your America, try one of the remaining railroad lines before the buses and airplanes take over completely. Don't try to know your country by automobile, because the highways are exactly the same coming into and leaving each town as they are with any other. There is a continuous stretch of supermarkets and roadside stores wherever you want to go. And don't use the airlines, for you will fly over the richness of American countryside without seeing or feeling or smelling it. You should see at least one face from each state you go through. Travel, to me, is more than getting from here to there.

You forget automobile and airplane trips, but an old-time train trip was like an ocean voyage, with tears and goodbye-waving, candy and magazines. The music of the rails and the sounds of the dining car and the bells and wailing of the train as it sped through the night are rich memories that I wish all the people of today and tomorrow might have known.

Every now and then, someone asks why I use pressed-wood Masonite for my paintings and before I can reply, my memories go way back to my youth and a ride I hitched to Taos, New Mexico, with a disgruntled and not too sober lumber salesman. I threw my sign-painting kit in the back of his car, on top of a heap of sample boards. "I've had this job for two years," the man said, "and after I've made this call, I'm going back to Santa Fe and quit. Never, under any condition," he continued, "take a job selling lumber! Especially out in this country."

For a young fellow who had run away from home and earned his way as best he could, any advice was welcome and taken seriously. But having made my way that far as a sign painter, I decided that being a serious painter was for me. And the then new bohemia of American painters, the Indian village town of Taos, seemed a fine place to start.

By the time we arrived at Taos, the lumber salesman and I had done some considerable talking and had become very well acquainted. When we parted, he called me back to his car. "I know you're making signs, young fellow," he said, "and I think you might find good use for these sample boards. My company just invented them; they thought they might sell them for some kind of building boards, and I don't think they're wrong. I'm quitting this job, so if you can use these sample boards for making signs, you're welcome to them."

Those slabs of Masonite, back in 1925, were used not only by me but by some of the famous western artists like Couse and Berninghouse and Gaspard;

and they started a nationwide trend. Nowadays, almost half of the paintings in America seem to be painted on the stuff, and the advantages are many.

One advantage is that you can cut a painting exactly as a photographer crops his pictures, which is difficult to do with canvas stretched on a frame. One of my favorite anecdotes concerns a painting of mine that was damaged on its way to California, arriving there with a four-inch hole right through the middle. I sawed the thing about in half and kept one half in my studio until a lady knocked at my door one day. "I saw that 'half a picture,'" she said, "and I've fallen in love with it. I know you had sold the original for four thousand dollars, so I want to buy the half for two thousand. Here's my check."

Another Masonite anecdote arose when a friend picked up a painting for an art show in Meriden, Connecticut. Within a few minutes, however, he returned sadly, saying that he'd just realized the picture was too big, larger than the regulation proportions allowed for that show. "Your painting, with the frame," he said, "is fifty inches, and the limit is supposed to be only forty inches."

"Oh, don't let that worry you," I said. "Come on in for a moment and I'll put a pot of tea on." Then I began taking the picture out of the frame. As my friend was sipping his tea, I sawed my painting to the correct size, sawed down the frame, and in a while he went off with a regulation-size entry. You can't do that sort of thing with a canvas. "Damndest performance I ever saw," said my friend.

Sawing paintings might sound ridiculous, but I never really plan a picture. I try to "let it paint itself," and my saw is sometimes as much a tool as my paintbrushes. I never did like plans anyway.

Perhaps one thing that soured me on plans was when I built my own garage. I measured my automobile first, and then I added about two feet to all the measurements, back and front, left and right. Anyone would think there is nothing wrong with such a plan—it certainly looked fine on paper. But if you ever want to build a small garage, don't use my system. New car doors are over six inches thick, and you'll find you can drive your car in, but you can't open the doors enough to get out, and that isn't a good arrangement.

Returning to Masonite—the indestructibility of pressed wood is also an advantage, and not without its anecdotes. I recall many years ago when I told my friend Amy Vanderbilt that you could hammer or kick such a painting. A little while after our conversation, we heard Conga music and a loud banging. It seems her little boy had invited his friends over. "Come on over," he said. "We have a new picture you can hammer and kick." The painting survived quite a few Conga kicks.

the Painter's delight

I remember during prohibition days, when most life insurance companies shunned anyone who called himself an artist. We were supposed to lead a fast and dangerous life. Even a couple of decades ago when I moved to the country, I found that the painter's reputation did nothing to enhance the prospects of a mortgage or personal bank loan. They told me that in so many words. But now things have changed. I not only have a mortgage but I am considered a member of the human race. Today artists have crew cuts and the people who dress like the long-haired painters of two or three decades ago are considered perfectly normal.

When I first moved to the country, people expected something pretty unpredictable from a painter who moved into the neighborhood, and I didn't help that situation. I told my realtor that I wanted "a very secluded place," but he kept showing me houses with another farmhouse just a short way off. "Oh, they won't bother you," he'd tell me. "In the summer, when the trees are in leaf, you can hardly see the other house. This is really a most secluded type house."

How, I wondered, could I impress him with what I meant by "secluded"? At any rate, I tried. "Let me tell you, Mr. Curry," I said, "the kind of place I want. I want to be able to shoot off a gun without hitting a house next door. Have you got that?" He allowed as how he had it. "Then," I continued, "I want to be able to run around the house stark naked, without anyone seeing me." He allowed as how he understood that too, and I thought I had finally impressed him with the amount of privacy I expected when I said "seclusion." The only thing that I accomplished, however, was to get myself known throughout the countryside as "the crazy artist feller who runs around his house naked, shooting off guns."

I think I won over most of the local country people though, by my decision to paint barns. Most artists, they said, painted women; but a fellow who paints barns must be "pretty normal like." I even got invitations now and then for supper. Soon I got to be known as "that barn painter" which set off an epidemic of telephone calls. "I understand you paint barns," they would say. "I guess I do," I'd reply. "Well, my barn hasn't been painted in years now, and I've heard you do pretty good work. You've got the job if the price is right."

When I first started portraying barns in Connecticut, most of the barns were those very long red tobacco barns, and I wondered why I sold the pictures so quickly. Even before the paint was dry, if the picture featured a very long red barn, it was sold almost under my nose. Then I got a little curious. "Why did you buy two of these paintings?" I asked one of the buyers. "Oh, I just love covered bridges," she said.

That was when I decided I'd paint covered bridges for a living and from then on, if all the covered bridges I've painted were put end to end, they would equal the length of all the real covered bridges layed end to end. It was great fun, but I've painted my last covered bridge. My bridge period is done with. About fifteen years ago when I painted my first covered bridge (and wrote *American Barns and Covered Bridges*), there were some two thousand covered bridges in America. The state that had the most was Pennsylvania, then came Ohio, Indiana, Oregon and, last, Vermont. Today I might guess only half (or less) are left. If, during my bridge period, I missed painting or sketching any one of them, I want to apologize. They were good to me.

I don't like trading stamps or premiums.

My dog Spookie disagrees with my way of thinking, but maybe you are different. First I'd like to explain that, on my way back from the city, I usually buy a whole liverwurst for Spookie, and that's the only way I can partly make up for not having taken him along with me. Well, the last time I came home without a liverwurst I tried to explain "why" in dog language, but it didn't work. The only store open had liverwurst that came in a package with a yo-yo premium, and as I happened to be against premiums and gift "come-ons," I left empty handed.

My wife sort of agreed with Spookie, who intimated he wouldn't mind what came with the liverwurst so long as he received it. Ruth said she heard how the poor yo-yo company had been failing, and how maybe the idea was a way to help the yo-yo company get back on its feet. I said I'd be glad to help the company to get back on its feet by buying a yo-yo, but if yo-yos came with gift liverwursts, the deal would be off.

My premiumitis started with those Cracker Jack packages that have a toy prize inside them. It was when I almost ate a plastic jumping jack that I first acquired my dislike for premiums, but it got worse when, after pouring some cereal into a dish of cream, I found a Man From Mars in it. A disgusting little fellow. Now, however, housewives seem to shop only where they can get toys, free towels, pansy seeds, and drinking glasses along with boxes of food. Once I saw a lady buying something with a strange new name that I think was "Instant Whange." The name intrigued me and I asked the lady what Instant

[81]

Whange was. "I don't really know," she said, "but my little boy loves balloons." Then I saw that there was a package of balloons with each package.

Another pet dislike of mine is the stuff marked TEN CENTS OFF! in letters twice the size of the name itself. Of course the idea is the old merchandising gimmick that the average person would buy a dozen elephants if there was enough of a discount. But as soon as I see one of those discount signs on something (even if I really need it) I go out of my way not to buy it, just as I do with free premiums. I've eaten enough free coupons and gift toys, and I'm sorry to force Spookie to go along with my pet peeves, but yo-yos with liverwurst was going too far.

Recently I dined at an inn and sat right beneath a big lithographed reproduction of an Eric Sloane painting. "Looks good, doesn't it?" said the proprietor. "I got it with premium stamps. As a matter of fact, they came with the very order of corned beef hash that you are eating." The hash all of a sudden didn't taste so good. "I think I'd rather have the fried chicken," I said.

Later, I complained to the man who makes the lithographs, and he said that sort of thing doesn't harm my status at all. "We give out Picassos and Rembrandts too," he explained. So I guess I felt better about it. Maybe I will become brainwashed by this kind of merchandising and give away trading stamps with the sale of original paintings.

The early American premium started out as a respected item, like the bag that store-bought flour was sold in. It was made of gingham or printed cotton, and every farmer's wife could hardly wait to empty the flour bag, wash and iron it, and make a new housedress out of it. Then there was the blue paper that loaf-sugar was wrapped in; it was this paper, boiled in water, that gave the old-time farmer's wife her blue dye.

The first modern type premium was introduced by Benjamin Talbert Babbitt in 1865 when he sold the first wrapped soap. People at once complained that they were "paying for the paper wrapping," so he just printed the word "coupon" on the wrappers and gave a "beautiful lithograph" for ten of them. What havoc he began!

the Germans liked any color...
...as long as it was *Red*

Father-in-laws (or is it fathers-in-law?) have a knack of asking embarrassing questions. "Why," asked mine, "did you buy the house next door if you didn't even like it?" Of course, if he hadn't been my father-in-law, I don't know if I could have admitted I only bought it because I didn't like the color and just wanted to repaint it. Most people wouldn't understand that sort of logic.

It seems that the original owner (who was in Switzerland) ordered the caretaker (in German) to paint the house "like a fire-engine." I guess she didn't know how to say "red" in English, and you know how those German people like similes. Anyway, the caretaker, who follows orders to the letter, sent to the La France Fire Engine Company for a lot of red enamel, and when he got through painting the house with that, whoever looked at the sight was compelled to say, "Wow!"

My own home became known as "the place next to the red house." Although I have since bought the place and repainted it a dull gray, the oil bills still are addressed to "the red house." Even the painter who put on the new gray paint sent me a bill for "painting the red house." There is something about a red building in New England that endears itself to the beholder, but this job was too much. I have several flying friends who make a habit of buzzing my place when they pass within range, and they all say they had no difficulty picking it out. "That red house next door is like a beacon," they used to tell me.

In the beginning, New England houses were always unpainted. Those "little white colonial villages" you read about are nothing but movie-set inventions. To paint your house at all was considered vulgar, but to paint your barn was even worse—it would win you the contempt of every farmer for miles around. Until the 1800's, even a weathervane was considered decoration in bad taste.

It was in Pennsylvania, where they liked "to make pretty the things they were most proud of," that the first painting of barns began, and the addition of huge barn weathervanes started. That was way back around 1840. The painted barn wasn't accepted in New England until long after the Civil War, and even then the paint work began on the *inside* with white paint made of milk. Oddly enough, milk will still make the best plastic paint, outlasting most other kinds. If you put a pound of salt and ten pounds of lime into a gallon of milk you will get an early American white barn paint. Legend has it that they used blood to make the red color but that isn't true. Farmstock blood was used for staining and dying, and for some inside paints too, but not for outside barn paint. It was when oxide of iron ground in oil became a base that the red barns were born. The standard "solid red" mixture was:

6 pounds of Venetian Red (35 percent sesquioxide of iron ground in oil)
1 pound of resin
2 gallons (or 3) of raw linseed oil.

At first, only the south side of the old barns was painted, with the reason that dark red accepts the sun's rays quicker than shiny raw wood, and also so that the barn might be better heated in winter. Likewise, the inside white paint had its non-decorative reason for being. The early barn used to have few or no windows, and the illuminating quality of white paint made vision inside the barn a great deal easier.

But the oldest wooden buildings in America are still those that were never painted. Perhaps some day the art of seasoning lumber will return, and people will again enjoy the richness of weathered, unpainted wood.

the Nutmeg flag

If you enjoy words, the flag above might interest you. It is the flag of the Island of Grenada that was known first for its pomegranates and nutmegs. Grenada, to begin with, was the French word for pomegranate, taken from the Latin *pomun grenatum* or "seedy apple." The pomegranate, it seems, has a great many seeds which nature, at the proper season, explodes outward.

When the French invented a bomb that exploded metal "seeds" outward, they called it a *pome grenate,* and the English-speaking soldiers who found that too much of a mouthful settled for "grenade." And of course the British bomb-throwers became "grenadiers." Romantically speaking, they threw pomegranates.

But the fruit on the flag above is not a pomegranate; it is the nutmeg made famous by the early American spice trade. This *mega* nut or *big* nut, was most popular in the American colonies and, at one time, was exchanged almost like currency because the nuts were so easy to carry in the pocket. With a pocketful of nutmegs you could get almost anything (in like value) at any store. Then, when the New Englander became famous for being a traveling salesman, people began to notice that he always had a pocketful (or pocketsful) of the spicy nuts, and so the Yankee peddler got the name of "nutmegger."

Nutmegs were carried in ladies' handbags and gentlemen carried them in little nutmeg-boxes. When you "dined out" or "drank out," it was stylish to carry your own nutmeg-grater and pass that spice around for hot toddies and tea cakes. There were probably hundreds of designs of personal nutmeg-graters, but the modern type standard design made all the gadgetty ones obsolete, and they have become rare antique items now. A favorite early American Christmas gift was a painted or gilded nutmeg, with a tiny greeting lettered on it, and such nutmegs were tied to our earliest Christmas trees, with ribbons attached.

The famed "wooden nutmegs" of Yankee history began late (during the Civil War), when Yankee prisoners idled their time away by carving from wood. It seemed easy and at least amusing to carve what resembled a nutmeg. But it is doubtful that a peddler ever offered wooden nutmegs for sale except as a joke.

I often wonder about the worth of such trivia, but the fun of unearthing knowledge is at least entertaining. I was surprised and amused to learn, for example, that the nutmeg trade was responsible for the American suspender. In 1798, the American shipping firm of Webb and Lamb decided to corner the market in nutmegs, and they filled a ship with more nutmegs than had been seen in years, ready to sail for New England after they had created a nutmeg shortage there. The plan failed, however, as the ship was wrecked and Mr. Lamb was drowned. And from that time on, the nutmeg business in America began to dwindle.

Oh yes—about the suspenders. Mr. Orange Webb, who had lost his partner and all of his money, patented a strap "for holding up the breeches or pantaloons" and on that day (September 18, 1804), the American suspender was born. The first sale was to the New York Fire Department—two hundred red suspenders. Somehow or other, the name "Orange Webb" sounded exactly like the red webbed-rubber straps that they were, and the Orange Webb Suspender became known all over the world. Mr. Orange Webb, along with a lot of other Yankees, forgot about nutmegs.

...the column that put me in the

My dog feels the same way about cats as I do: we can take them or leave them. But Spookie and I can't understand why some people look starry-eyed and choke up at the mere mention of the word "cat." I guess Spookie is just a man dog and I'm a dog man. Occasionally, though, we can't help but feel sorry for cats. There are so many dogs and people who look down on the cat world. Even the word "cat" (from the Greek prefix *kata*) means "down," as in "cataract" (which rushes down), the "catacombs" (which are dug down) and catechism (which is sounded down). And man did go awfully far to find a suitable, noble name for his canine pet—imagine turning the name of God backwards! It wasn't fair.

Sometimes you find people who feel so sorry for cats that they collect them by the dozens. Ask why they like cats so, and they start by telling you how independent cats are. Well, to me, that rules them out as pets, because I think being dependent is exactly what makes a pet a pet. Dependence is what makes a friend a friend, or a man and woman one. When your lion gets too independent he usually eats you.

Then they'll tell you how graceful cats are. I guess my cat is graceful when he catches a bird but I think birds are graceful, too. Sometimes my cat pounces on a mouse, but I happen to like mice. My cat sleeps most of the time and when he goes to his eating dish he trots like a little horse.

[87]

"This," said my wife, Ruth, "is one hell of a column! Don't you know that you're going to lose a lot of readers? I happen to like cats very much, and so do other people. I like dogs too but I don't go around knocking other people's likes or dislikes. I'll bet there are readers who don't like dogs and might want to know what you think is so great about them."

Well, if that be so, may I say that I've never seen a Seeing Eye cat. I've never known a cat you could go walking or hunting with, or a cat that finds lost mountain climbers and carries a rum-cask around its neck. I've never seen a cat that herds cattle or pulls sleds or chases burglars or saves drowning children or rides a hook-and-ladder.

I guess my dog and I get along because we are slaves to each other's wishes. We have a reverence for dependency. We think dependency is what makes the world go 'round and sparks the wonderful art of faithfulness.

The other day, when I wanted to go to the city and take my dog along, I phoned the Howard Johnson hotel there. I'd heard that they accepted dogs. "Do you?" I asked the manager. "Well," he replied, "I never heard of a dog who smoked in bed. I've never known a dog to go away without paying or a dog who took along some of the hotel linen. I'd say your dog is very welcome. Just have him register."

That was the best word I'd heard in honor of dogdom since Lord Byron wrote the epitaph for his Newfoundland:

Beneath this spot are deposited the remains of a being who was possessed of beauty without vanity, strength without insolence, courage without ferocity, and all the virtues of man without man's vices.

P.S.: My wife made me promise I'd give equal time to cats, and someday I will.

Sign of the Handyman

They say that specialization began with the trade sign. But there was one early trade sign that advertised the non-specialist: a big wooden hand—the sign of the handyman.

Someone phoned me recently and asked if I knew where to find a good handyman. "I looked through the Yellow Pages and couldn't find any such listing," he said. "Has the handyman vanished as a profession?" It made me think.

I recalled that when I was a boy—back in the non-union days—there were lots of handymen and they were always busy. They did everything, from digging holes to building and carpentry. Nowadays, however, the word "handyman" has a sad and forlorn sound. Little boys no longer say "when I grow up I'd like to be a handyman." But if I could pick someone to be stranded with on a desert island I'd choose a handyman all right, or maybe a handygirl. And I'd like to salute a real credit to mankind—that rare fellow who can do a little bit of everything.

My handyman, who prefers to call himself a "house doctor," is worth his weight in gold. Not that he works so hard but he is always handy to make me either laugh or think. And if you are a practical jokester and you live in the New England countryside, it isn't easy to have a fall-guy handy at all times. Harley is still puzzled by my reverence for old weather-beaten barn wood and old rusty handmade nails. He wonders why I eat off an ancient, but well-polished barn door set on legs. "I just got a nice plastic-topped table with green stamps," he told a neighbor, "and offered it to Sloane. But he says he likes his barn-door table better. City folks have funny ideas."

A flying friend dropped by a few weeks back, during a rainstorm, and I lent him a dry suit to wear home. Yesterday he passed by in his airplane and he tossed the borrowed suit, bundled up, out of the plane. It sailed nicely into my pasture, where an amazed Harley picked it up and then brought it to me. "Look at this!" he said. "I know," I replied casually. "That was just my dry-cleaning man. He always delivers my orders that way."

Another reason Harley puzzles over me is that the gift I most like to receive is a bundle of old rags. To a painter who uses them in his painting technique, rags can be a most welcome thing. So when anyone asks me what I want for my birthday or for Christmas, the answer is always rags. They can be gift wrapped or not, but they must have aesthetic value. Some of my neighbors bring me just any old rags, and when I hang an old brassiere or a pair of worn-out corduroy pants on my easel, it does something to my work. It just isn't inspiring. But give me a mess of torn clean sheets and a few paints and the picture is most likely to turn out worthy of Eric Sloane, A.N.A.

Then too, Harley is a punster—I think. Or maybe it's just New England language. He told me about the *Kosher Nostre,* which he insists is the Jewish Mafia, and while I'm not sure, I'll have to give him credit for a clever pun.

I was convinced that he had a good sense of humor when I took the label off a can of my spray varnish and put it on his can of window-washing spray, and then asked him to clean the windows in my studio with it. I didn't have the joy of seeing him discover my joke and he never said a word about it. But a week later when I sprayed one of my oil paintings with window-washing spray, I knew he had turned the tables on me. I think maybe I'll fire him.

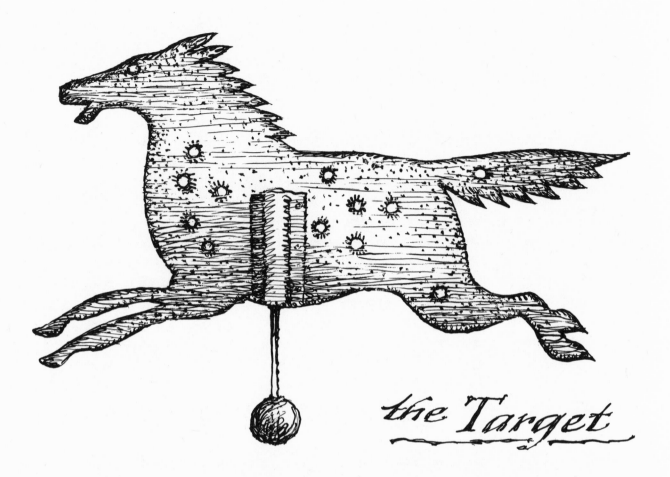

the Target

One of the handicaps of being an author is the avalanche of letters that begin, "Why don't you write a book about . . . ?" I guess I've received thousands of such suggestions. They're never exciting, such as books about women, but always proposals for books on iron mines, glass-making, or early trinkets and gadgets. When you write one successful book, people want you to do the same thing, over and over. Of course the secret of success is to resist it.

I was reminded of all this when I received a letter today that began, "Why don't you do a book about weather vanes?" and it carried me way back to the first Americana book I ever wrote. That was when most of my mail began "Dear Mr. Sloane, Unless . . ." and I guess I just had less resistance in those days.

I was called in to the old Funk & Wagnalls office, and because of my interest in weather, they thought I was the one to do a book about weather vanes. "I don't think there would be enough of a sale," I said, "but why not a book about covered bridges? Everyone loves a covered bridge. I have a friend named Richard Allen who is an expert on covered bridges and he can do it for you."

"But we've already made out a contract for a book on weather vanes by you," they said. "And even a check for advance royalties." It was then that I remembered my stack of mail that started with the word "unless."

"Tell you what," I said. "If you cross out the title about weather vanes and put in one about covered bridges, I'll sign that contract. And take that check."

That was how my Americana list started, and every time one book was done the publisher said, "That's fine. Now do another." After repeating myself so cleverly that nobody knew the difference between any of them, I threw up my hands. "No more Americana books!" I said. "I'm fresh out of ideas."

"But what are we going to do for next year?" they asked.

"Why don't you put my last three books in a box and sell them as a set?"

It sounded silly at first, but they did just that, and everyone who had the three books couldn't resist buying another three just because they were now in a box. People like "sets" of things. I had a friend who was going out of business trying to sell little cans of maple syrup. Then he put three cans in a little box tied with a red ribbon and they sold like the hot-cakes they would go on. It's the American way.

But I still get requests for a book about weather vanes, and I wonder what there is about weather vanes that so many people enjoy. I guess it is their antiquity. Or the fact that they bring such amazing prices in the antique shops. The price of one I noticed recently happened to be the exact amount that I once paid for a new automobile. "Those bullet holes," the salesman said, "were made by Revolutionary soldiers."

All old weather vanes have bullet holes in them, but the story about soldiers making them is just a happy myth. Soldiers with the old-time rifles were too thrifty with their powder and shot. But if you were ever a little boy with a new gun, you'll know how those bullet holes got there. What better target than a rooster, sitting on a church spire, waiting to be spun around?

I guess there are a lot of myths and enough anecdotes about weather vanes to make a good book but I'd still rather keep it as "the one I'll never write." I have an old weather vane on the roof above me as I write these words, and it creaks and groans every time the wind changes; it's an old friend who constantly remarks about the weather, and every time I look at it I have an excuse for looking upward. "What a fine lamp you could make out of that weather vane," someone said recently. "With a shade on your head," I replied, "you'd make a good lamp too."

the First Paper Bag
Pat. 65,176   May 28, 1867

A historian's lot is sometimes an unhappy one. For instance, last night I saw a TV show that featured Abraham Lincoln as a storekeeper. He sold a lady some candy and said, "Here—I'll put it in a bag for you." The very small fact that bags were at first called "pokes" and that the first paper bag hadn't been invented yet caused me just enough concern to shatter the illusion of an otherwise convincing play. My favorite mood-shattering scene, however, was a TV presentation of Lincoln's arrival at Gettysburg. I distinctly heard an extra in the crowd scene make the mistake of shouting, "Hurrah for Mr. Massey."

It is unimportant trivia to know that the Stars and Stripes were not carried in battle until the period of the Mexican War, but when I see a Revolutionary battle portrayed with Old Glory waving, I begin to lose interest. Even Emanuel Leutze's great painting of Washington crossing the Delaware loses its appeal for me when I see the Stars and Stripes, which had not yet been designed. Of course, thirteen men in a twelve-foot boat is a bit incredible anyway.

In one movie I saw a Revolutionary soldier fold the Stars and Stripes as we do now, into a triangle. And according to historical legend, that custom began much later. But maybe you'd like to hear that story, and also learn how the flag got to be called "Old Glory."

The story goes that a Salem sea captain named William Driver was presented by his minister with an American flag for his ship. "Each corner," said the minister, "has been folded in the name of the Holy Trinity; and each mention of Father, Son, and Holy Ghost was acclaimed by the congregation with a response of 'Glory, glory, glory.' So when you fold this flag, wherever you are, fold it so, and remember the faith of your religion that has made your nation great."

Captain Driver remembered this, and was so impressed that with each fold, he commanded his crew to respond with "Glory!" Captain Driver and his

"Old Glory" became quite famous on the high seas, until the old captain retired and went to live in Nashville, Tennessee. Then, during the Civil War, when the city was captured by General Grant, there was a call for a large American flag to replace the Confederate one that had flown over the state capitol, and Driver's "Old Glory" was chosen. Grant (according to the legend) was so impressed with the story that he ordered all army flags to be folded in the same manner from that time on.

The grand old Betsy Ross legend still persists, even in our schoolbooks, although there is much evidence that she didn't design our flag. Francis Hopkinson (a signer of the Declaration of Independence) sent a bill for having designed the Stars and Stripes, and a board refused to pay it only because "Hopkinson was not the only person involved, and he was already being paid as a member of the Congress." He also sent a bill "for having designed the Great Seal of the United States of America, with a Reverse"—those designs shown on the back of a dollar bill.

And while we are in a mood of trivia, that Great Seal design with the pyramid on it was never used anywhere officially except on the dollar bill. The eye atop the unfinished pyramid is the "Eternal Eye of God," and the pyramid built of thirteen layers represents the strength of the original Union. The date at the bottom is 1776 and the motto *Novus Ordo Seclorum* means A New Order of the Ages. The motto on top (*Annuit Cooptis*) means He Has Favored Our Undertaking. As a national emblem and part of the Great Seal of The United States of America, it is probably the least-known design even though it is on every dollar bill.

To prove my point, I asked my wife, "What do you know about the Great Seal of the United States?" Ruth either has a keener wit of late, or she was caught off guard. "I thought," she replied, "that the great seal was extinct. Or are there still some left in Alaska?"

I have never heard it discussed historically, but people used to have a closer association with death than they do now. Mention the word "death" nowadays and you will be shushed in the average conversation. It is a subject we just don't want to consider. Guests at William Randolph Hearst's San Simeon estate were instructed never to mention death. Only a century or so ago, however, even small children were taught to think about death as much or even more than life. Even the bed-time prayer ended, "If I should die before I wake . . ." and little girls wrote poems on their sewn samplers about death. Graveyards were parks and, somehow or other, although people didn't live as long, memories of them lasted longer than they do now.

As far as I'm concerned, no guest room is complete without some sort of comic epitaph book. And if you compare the numerous publications, you will soon find that authors have added, embellished, or often made up some of their own versions. I've never found a gravestone very comical, but I was partly won over when I moved to a country house and found that my marble patio was actually made of old tombstones turned face down. Of course I turned them all right side up, and provided my place with conversation material. One lady asked that I change places with her. "I don't feel comfortable with my

[95]

chair on this stone," she said. "It is the tombstone of my great-grandmother."

Perhaps Sir Thomas More started the comic epitaph when he wrote one at the urgent entreaty of a Susan Blake:

GOOD SUSAN BLAKE IN ROYAL STATE
ARRIVED AT LAST AT HEAVEN'S GATE.

Then after a number of years and a falling out with her, he added:

BUT PETER MET HER WITH A CLUB
AND SENT HER BACK TO BEELZEBUB.

In the late 1700's there was a fad for composing one's own epitaph, and although the whole thing was done in jest, when the person died there was always a chance the joke would be taken seriously. This resulted in the many quaint poems you may still see on the Early American grave-markers. They were seldom if ever composed by anyone but the deceased. Here are some samples:

I ROGER SMITH BENEATH THIS TOMB
IN SIXTY YEARS HAVE REACHED MY DOOM.
AND NEVER MARRIED, THINK IT SAD
AND WISH MY FATHER NEVER HAD

HERE LIES ANN MANN
SHE LIVED AN OLD MAID
BUT DIED AN OLD MANN

MY NAME IS JOHN KEITH
I USED TO PULL TEETH
BUT VIEW ME WITH GRAVITY
I'VE FILLED MY LAST CAVITY

HERE LIES THE COOPER RICHARD THOMAS, NOW FOOD FOR WORMS
LIKE AN OLD RUM PUNCHEON WHOSE STAVES ARE ALL MARKED AND NUMBERED
HE WILL BE RAISED AND PUT TOGETHER BY HIS MAKER

Then there were stock epitaphs which the stone carver supplied when a tombstone was ordered and paid for before death. A favorite that appears many times and in many places, is:

REMEMBER ME AS YOU PASS BY:
AS YOU ARE NOW SO ONCE WAS I.
AS I AM NOW SO YOU MUST BE:
PREPARE FOR DEATH AND FOLLOW ME.

To this, one stone-cutter added:

TO FOLLOW YOU I'M NOT CONTENT
TILL I FIND OUT WHICH WAY YOU WENT.

When a church looked like a church.

In this age when men strive to look like women and women to look like men, good taste and tradition are becoming obsolete. It might be said that things that look like what they are tend to be unfashionable.

I remember when I hired a local farmer to help me make an outdoor patio. "For the life of me," he grumbled, "I can't see why anyone would want to eat in the midst of the wind and the flies. City folks have funny ideas. We used to eat inside and go to the toilet outside; now they go to the toilet inside and eat outside."

And so things change without our realizing it—even the architecture of our homes. The old house shape divided into proper rooms is already a thing of the past. Now the architect arranges rooms like he would blocks, usually in a most complicated and unlikely shape; then he throws a tent of plywood and two-by-fours over that shape. The bathroom, however, must be *properly* placed

[97]

(backing up against the kitchen piping and sewage lines). In fact it is the only room that demands such special placement, and, as a result, it's fair to say the thing we used to put out in the back yard is now the nucleus of American home architecture.

Along with that piece of perfection, the American saltbox, the traditional American church is also disappearing. That is logical because traditional American religion is disappearing too.

When America was young (things get old quickly nowadays, you know) every village was built around a green and a church. Now the American village is built around a bank. Shopping centers become the center of a new village as soon as a bank joins that complex of buildings. I've yet to see a church claiming this important modern position and function. Banking is obviously presumed to be a more important institution than religion in the American scene.

The word "inspire" always came to my mind when I approached a New England village and saw its identifying church spire. But nowadays an architect wouldn't know how to go about making a proper spire. Have you seen those new apologies for church spires? Sometimes they are attempts to modernize the spire idea and sometimes they are just trying to be economical, but the spire always ends up looking like a bad cartoon. The spire of one new college building rests on four fins exactly like a poised rocket. Then there are modern churches built like something from Expo 67 or like big roadside custard stands. Little spires are tacked on as afterthoughts, just to make sure people will know they are looking at what is supposed to be a church. Art and architecture, I suppose, change along with artists and architects. And churches change with religion.

One story that makes me think is about a class of student artists and architects that had a costume dance. One student had particularly long, red whiskers that made him look like the Saviour. "Why don't you go dressed as the Lord?" someone asked him. It sounded good to him, so he dressed in a loincloth and built a large wooden cross. Then he waited outside his house to be picked up by a fellow student who had a car. But the fellow student weakened at the last moment and decided to have no part in it. So the whiskered student put his cross on his shoulders and began the trek to the masquerade.

It wasn't long before a police patrol spotted him, and took him, along with his cross, to the police station. But it seems he hadn't violated any particular law—only good taste and respect for religion. And there is no law that demands respect for religion. Or good taste either.

the Heritage of Age

A good painting should stand on its merits without a frame, and some day I'd like to have an exhibition of frameless pictures. Those big, old-time fancy gold frames are still sought for mirrors, but we have been educated almost enough to recognize them as little more than a detraction from a good painting.

Yet people still want "appropriate frames" and I'm still trying to find them. Recently I bought my fifth old barn—and old barns are indeed part of America's heritage. I wanted some of the old siding for the kind of frame wood that buyers prize for their barn paintings. One company manufactures "Early American frames" with worm holes. "Gives your painting the American Heritage look," states the brochure. And the way we take that sort of thing for granted makes you think—or at least it should.

There's a lot of loose talk about the American heritage which makes it sound like a national attic of obsolete trivia. Anything ancient, from a chamber pot to a wooden icebox, qualifies as "Americana" nowadays, and just because of its age and obsolescence, it is supposed to be treated with reverence. If you aren't aware of this, just look into the average antique shop—which once sold works of art—and you'll find it more resembles the old-time junk shop.

Now that "Early American" has become a phrase of reverence, and anything old and obsolete has sudden artistic and nostalgic value, the town dump has become an important American establishment. Not everyone is aware of it, but each dump is now presided over by a dump-master and there is a gate, with "hours of admittance" posted on it. That makes it difficult for a lot of antique dealers who used to get so much of their merchandise from the dumps. I discarded an old wooden bench and it was picked up by the local garbage man. A year later I bought it back, not recognizing it at first, after a dealer had scraped it down nicely.

Once I bought a round pine table through a mail-order advertisement that described the table as "Early American." When it arrived, however, I found it disappointing, so I swapped it at an antique shop for a weather vane. The dealer beat the table with a chain, shot it with "worm holes," mellowed it with a blowtorch, and sold it at a fine profit. A few days ago my eyes lit on a table in a friend's home and I recognized it as my fifty-dollar mail-order buy. "It's a genuine heritage piece," my friend told me. "At four hundred dollars, it's an investment." By adding artificial age, an artificial heritage was also added. At least three hundred and fifty dollars' worth.

The only worthwhile thing about age is that it affords more time for learning and for good deeds. If you don't learn anything or do any good works, old age will do for you only what it does for a dead fish—maybe a little slower. Speaking as an antiquarian and philosopher, may I say, "phooey on age." The heritage of age is a sad and crippling one.

I have a book called *A Modern Guide to Good Health,* written in 1780, and the first part of it tells how to make sassafras tea, how sweet fern soothes and alder bush heals, and how to use all sorts of wild herbs. How wonderful it must have been in those days, I thought. Then I turned to the second part, which tells how to deal with cholera and set false teeth. It also gives instructions, step by step, how to amputate arms and legs using common kitchen implements. Most ailments, it explains, call for immediate bleeding, and the worse the ailment the more copious should be the bleeding. Natural bleeding was stopped by "a mortar of cobwebs and ground roots." If the nose bleeds, fill a pig's gut with vinegar and stuff it gently up the victim's nostril." Good old days indeed. I can be thankful that the Maker saw fit to let me do my act in this century.

Actually, if you seek Americana in the antique shop, what you'll usually find is in the form of European and early English tradition and craftsmanship. And the real American heritage will be ignored, for the American heritage has no antique value; its value is right now. It is the tradition of design, the excellence of workmanship, the honesty of value, the usefulness of simplicity, the reverence for nature and God. You'll find all these things in genuine Early Americana, and these are the things that give it value. Their age? That doesn't add a thing!

table

easel

bed

. . a box full of memories . .

"That wooden box you keep your drawings in," said my wife, "would make a good picnic table if you opened it and put legs on it." I guess Ruth had forgotten, or maybe I never told her the story. After all, it was fifty years ago, long before she was born. But the box really did begin as a picnic table.

When I ran away from home as a little fellow, I decided the table (which folded into a flat box, with a handle on top) would be just the thing to carry my clothes and the materials I needed for making signs and showcards. I was indeed right, for it also half-folded into a good easel, made a flat surface for my advertisement reading *"SIGNS MADE WHILE YOU WAIT,"* and more than a few times it opened up into a flat surface for sleeping on, in barns or out under the stars. I guess I've grown a great deal, for I tried to lie down on it now, and I don't fit.

But I'd really forgotten where the box came from, and Ruth's suggestion carried me back to hitchhiking on dirt roads in cars like Maxwells and Pierce-Arrows and Locomobiles. Nowadays I can't tell the difference between a Ford and a Lincoln because most cars look alike and at a quick glance you can't even tell the back from the front. On the inside of my nostalgic box, I had written down the names of the automobiles that were born in the one year of my away-from-home adventure, and although some of the wonderful names make my heart beat a little faster, I doubt that you can recall the Acorn, Ajax, Backhus,

Bauer, Diana, Harris, Julian, Majestic, Morrissey, and Titan Vim. Going out of business that same year were the Anderson, Apperson Jack Rabbit, Brewster, Columbia, Dagmar, Dorris, Dort, Fox, Gray, Haynes, H.C.S., Jewett, Lexington, Maxwell, Mercer, Owen-Magnetic, Premier, Stanley, Stephens, Westcott, and the Wills St. Clair.

With so many kinds of automobiles, a youngster's life was filled with the wonder and individualism of automotive design and it was a constant game to spot your favorite cars as they went past. Some cars you could even recognize by the sounds they made.

I guess what I miss most about the old-time automobiles is height. Nowadays when you go cross-country, your view is mostly confined to the gutter and to the immediate roadside. And if you want to win a bet, ask anyone how high the modern cartop or station wagon is. If the average man stretches his arm to a horizontal position, the car would still fit under it. My Model T roadster is six foot eleven inches high!

My 1929 Model A station wagon is too high to get into my garage, so I had to cut a piece from the building. But when I drive to town in it, I always have a fine view of the landscape, making each trip an extraordinary pleasure. When one of those expensive low-slung sportscars go past, I always feel sorry for the passengers groveling along in the dust. Their height also puts them in an embarrassing position; dogs have such contempt for automobile tires.

Once I bought a low-looking underslung Packard (remember the Packard?) and after I got a few miles from the used-car lot, I realized it wasn't underslung at all: the springs were broken! But being young and foolish, I didn't worry too much—anyway, I liked the low underslung look. The only trouble was that the car couldn't turn to the left without the tires hitting the fenders. But I found that you could make a sharp left turn simply by making two rights. Figure that one out for yourself. Anyway, I think I was the only one to travel from coast to coast without making a left turn.

"Litchfield" (Conn.)

mileage

"miles"

a Franklin stone.

The distance that people used to travel with few or no roads, have always amazed me. I thought about that recently when I saw near my neighborhood in New England, a granite milestone—one of many that were designated by the Postmaster General, who came all the way from Philadelphia in 1763 to do just that. He wasn't a very young man, and the work of accurately measuring out miles for the postman, and arranging for the stones to be cut, was work in itself. But traveling on Indian trails, footpaths, over dirt roads, and by flatboat and ferry for over two hundred miles in those days was considered no more than a trip to the store nowadays. And for so eminent and busy a person as Benjamin Franklin, such a performance makes you think.

Postage in the early days was paid for by the mile, and there had been complaints in New England about overcharges for postal transportation. Everyone's estimate of a mile was different and the postman often estimated a rough or an uphill distance of a mile as a mile and a half or even two. So Benjamin Franklin decided he would set a good and accurate example. He took his daughter Sally along, and she counted the revolutions of one of the wagon wheels, stopping at every mile and hammering in a wooden stake.

Now, when the post office is a money-losing proposition, and my mail box is crammed with advertising trash at the expense of the government, I wonder what has happened to the old time perseverance. I have a large container where

I deposit all unwanted and unordered catalogs and advertising mail, and each month I burn what always amounts to over fifty pounds of paper. That is over a quarter ton per year. In the old days you paid postage on a single sheet of paper, twice as much for two sheets and so on. I think this good arrangement should be revived for mail advertising, and I'll bet if Franklin were alive today he'd put it back into effect.

There were no mail boxes in Franklin's day, but a man's boot seemed to have something personal enough about it to identify it as a private depository for his mail, and indeed some of the first mail boxes in America were old boots. But rural delivery is not as old as most people believe. The first rural free delivery was established October 1, 1896, with three routes in West Virginia, and the system began to develop in the early 1900's.

Even envelopes are comparatively recent. Before 1840 all letters were written on one piece of paper which was folded and sealed, with the name and address written on the reverse blank side. The "outlook" or window envelope was invented in 1902. Even the word "mail" is comparatively new, for the dictionaries of the late 1700's give it the meaning of "a leather bag used for carrying letters" and so the "mail man" was a man who carried a leather bag. The word "post" is quite recent too, beginning with the eighteenth-century words "post-road," "post-rider," "outpost," and so on, all referring to the time when letters were carried by horsemen or post riders.

Franklin considered the General Post Office a non-profit business, but never a taxpayer's burden. By 1805 the post office rates started at eight cents for a single-sheet letter up to forty miles; up to ninety miles it was ten cents, and up to one hundred fifty miles it was twelve and a half cents. Up to three hundred miles the rate was seventeen cents, up to five hundred miles it was twenty cents and over five hundred miles it was twenty-five cents. Twenty-five cents in those days was a fair day's wage for a countryman.

Nowadays, when all kinds of transportation and telephone rates are on a distance basis, the post office will still send your mail anywhere in the nation at a flat sum and even help you sell your wares by mail, all at a staggering loss. But this is the age when we can "spend your way into prosperity" and Franklin's philosophy of saving is out of fashion. We have progressed into organizing the greatest postal service in the world, but at the greatest loss.

Perhaps our first Postmaster General had the right idea.

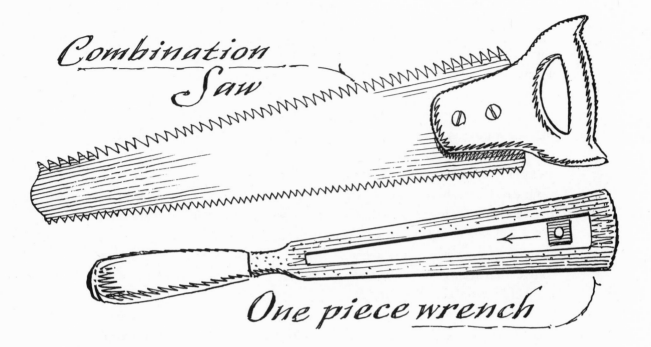

Combination Saw

One piece wrench

Above are two simple tools that were made over a century ago which I had installed in my small museum of early American implements. What is most interesting about them is that they are usually absent from the collection, because I am using them. Take that top tool for instance—it is a combination saw that has rip-teeth on one side of the blade and cross-cut teeth on the other. Why they aren't made now is a mystery. Furthermore, it's a saw that doesn't rust. You can leave it out in the rain, and because the metal was smelted with old-time charcoal (which hasn't the impurities of coal) it is rust-resistant.

Then take the lower tool, which is a common wrench. It is one-piece and so has no moving parts. It will fit almost any size nut; you just slide the slot over a nut until it is snug, and then turn it.

There were so many simple tools that were worthwhile, like the wooden mallet, which have disappeared. My handyman was hammering posts into the ground making a fence, and the sledge hammer he was using splintered the tops of the posts. Then he asked if he could borrow a big wooden "beatle" (mallet), and the job went along fine. Now, a beatle is a long-haired thing and a wooden mallet is an antique.

Every now and then (mostly now) the scissors that are supposed to be in the upper right-hand kitchen drawer (oh, yes—I'm that finicky) seem to disappear. "They are gone again!" I roared gently at my wife.

"If you look behind you," replied Ruth, "you will see a collection of early American scissors hanging on the wall as a decoration or 'utilitarian ornamentation' by an antiquarian character named Eric Sloane."

That was how I started using antique scissors, instead of just looking at them, and darned if they don't cut as well as the new ones! Maybe better. At least they always get hung back in place. Anyway, they gave me a special idea. People are always making lamps out of obsolete antiques and hanging "objets d'art" on their walls. Why not decorate your place with *usable* stuff? The idea of decorating a nook with a spinning wheel or the fireplace with a hanging bed-warmer has always seemed silly to me, unless you really spin flax or warm your bed before getting in. But if you can arrange kitchen tools attractively on your kitchen wall, voilà! Instant art!

Of course, you have to know what is attractive, but almost anything that is old and hand-made fits the bill. One of the first "placements" I made was a framed plaque of old wood with pegs for hanging my combination saw and my one-piece wrench. Then, when I sawed up a mess of firewood, I decided to pile it up against my studio wall decoratively. "What's better looking than a stack of firewood?" I asked Ruth.

She likes firewood but not that much. "You and your interior decoration ideas!" she said. "It looks all right in your old studio, but do stop giving people advice about decoration. Remember that dinner at the Caples."

Indeed I remembered. During dinner I noticed a fine large ancient painting which was so old and black that it was almost undistinguishable as a portrait. "Why don't you clean it?" I asked (instead of paying attention to my eating). "All you have to do is rub it with a sliced potato. Wait and I'll show you how."

After a few minutes of rubbing, I cleansed away a spot that turned out to be Great-grandmother Rosemarie's nose. It was beautifully pink, and it shined out from the blackness just like the day it was painted. "But you can't leave it that way!" my hostess lamented. "It looks awful. It's just a picture of a nose now!"

So after dinner I had to stay on till the wee hours finishing my job. It took six hours and twenty-two potatoes.

Butter stirrers

Apple Butter

There is an old saying that "there is nothing worse than pretty good violin playing." The New Englander had the same thing in mind when he said that "no good cook would own up to just pretty good apple butter." If you made apple butter at all, it had to be something sensational, a symphony of tastes and an identifying expression of the maker. About the same approach was required for home-made bread: if you can imagine hot home-made bread with fresh apple butter without your mouth watering, stop reading. It will be lost on you.

The early American did things to apples that just aren't done any more, and although people now look back upon them just as superstitions, the lack of these are what make modern-day cider and apple butter only "pretty good."

In the first place, half the art of apple-recipe lore was the science of apple bruising. Let me quote from an ancient book on the subject: "If the juice of the cider apple be extracted without first bruising the fruit, it will be found thin and defective in richness, compared to the juice of the same apple after it has been exposed to air and sunlight in a bruised state. It then becomes deeply tinged, less fluid and very rich. In its former state it apparently contained very little sugar; in the latter a great quantity. Even by bruising the apple more slowly, a difference in quality is again noticeable."

The modern method of grinding apples and immediately squeezing them makes a cider that great-grandfather wouldn't even accept as "pretty good." The same thing went for great-grandmother's apple butter, for she was a "bruiser" too. She carefully peeled, cored, and quartered the best of apples and then bruised them to just the right extent with a rolling-pin sort of implement. Squashing them into a pulp wasn't her intention. She then left them in their lumpy state on a bed of straw for exactly the time it took thirty gallons of good cider to boil down to fifteen gallons in a large kettle over an outdoor fire. During that time they "sugared" naturally. No cane sugar was used in the early American apple butter.

As soon as the cider was boiled down to half, four pails of apples were added, and the all-important stirring began. Because of the great heat and length of time required to make apple butter, the stirrers were often over twelve feet long, long enough for the stirrer to keep well away. They were made of sassafras wood, with no metal used. An expert stirrer could tell by the "feel" of it, when to add molasses (the only sweetening) and quinces and ground sassafras roots and whatever herbs the cook favored. The completion of apple butter called for a gathering of the family for official tasting on slabs of hot bread direct from the oven. What was left in the kettle after it had been emptied, by pouring hardened into "apple crisp," was reserved for the youngsters.

Perhaps apple butter made in the old way will come back again, but the time and care needed seem to make it a family affair rather than a commercial project. I am old enough to remember when peanut butter first appeared, and I recall that it came on the market along with date-nut butter. Date-nut butter was richer but there seemed to be less profit and commercial promise in it, so peanut butter stayed and prospered while date-nut butter disappeared. I even recall people making their own date-nut and peanut butter at home. If you pour plain roasted (shelled) peanuts into an electric mixer, you might be surprised to find what fine peanut butter results.

the Good old Days

It sounds strange, but things used to taste better and smell better than they do nowadays. There's a block-sized building down in New York where they do nothing but mix chemicals for adding to perfectly good food. They make bread smell more like bread, fruit jams taste like the fruit, and there isn't a spice or vegetable that they can't outsmell for you. There is almost no well-known packaged food producer today who doesn't do business with this company. I know of one who manufactures "pure mint jelly with pure artificial flavoring and pure artificial coloring." Without the added chemicals, they say, it would look and taste awful.

But every now and then you'll find an old-fashioned country store where your nose will momentarily forget its primary function of breathing, and enjoy the nearly lost art of smelling. The only thing that isn't doctored up in today's store seems to be ground coffee, and when you open one of those air-tight cans and the aroma flows out, you get a good idea of what I mean.

Being an antiquarian gives me the right to dwell in the past now and then, and to deplore the loss of trade names like Packard Automobiles and *Collier's* magazine, Zuzu Crackers and Gold Dust Cleanser. I even remember the old Sunday comics like *Little Nemo, Happy Hooligan, Buster Brown, Foxy Grandpa* and *Boob McNutt*. But there was one breakfast food that hit the spot. It was called Fortified Flakes, and it was crunchy but not too crunchy. For years I wondered what had become of that delight. And then I went to one of those health-food stores and while I was waiting for my crushed watercress juice, I spied a whole shelf full of Fortified Flakes.

"Fortified Flakes!" I cried aloud, and the proprietor dropped the glass of watercress juice. "So what?" he asked. "So I want to buy that whole shelf full," I answered, "I've been looking for that stuff for years!"

That night, I planned to recapture a bit of my past. On the way home I got some cream and brown sugar, and then I lit candles, built a fire in the fireplace, and set out my Fortified Flakes on the dinner table. With a feeling of nostalgic grandeur, I opened the box.

It wasn't the fact that moths flew out of the box that really amazed me. That only disgusted me. The real wonder was that these creatures had never before seen the light of day, had never breathed the outside air, and certainly had had no room to have done any flying. Yet without as much as a test-hop, they swarmed out like wartime aces and filled my room with their flapping wings. I opened box after box with the same result, until my room was a complete blizzard pattern.

Some weeks later, I went to the city and sought out my health-store friend.

"Do you remember me?" I asked. "Yes, indeed," he replied. "I'll never forget you. How were your Fortified Flakes?"

"What Fortified Flakes?" I said. "Those boxes were full of moths!" Of course I expected this statement to astonish him, but no. His eyes lit up and he pointed a commanding finger toward heaven. "See?" he cried. "See what?" I replied.

"Can't you see the wonder of it?" he went on. "Ordinary breakfast foods you buy nowadays wouldn't support life like that. Only Fortified Flakes had the vitamins and nourishment to create such a miracle. Isn't that wonderful?"

I have a sister in New Jersey who is another one of those health-via-vitamin buffs, and I could hardly wait to tell her this story. It would put her in her place, I thought, or at least give her a good laugh at herself. But when I got to the part where I opened the box and all the moths flew out, her eyes lit up. She pointed a commanding finger toward heaven and cried, "See?"

I knew what was coming, so I just gave up. You can't win with those vitamin-club members; they're as thick as black-strap molasses.

IT MAKES *you* THINK by Eric SLOANE

IT MAKES *you* THINK by SLO...

LL BRIDGE, Conn.
ME when I made a
...ting restaurant mu-
...one over the Roose-
...bar when that field
...mous airport. As I
...th water colors, I bor-
...nking glasses from
...ich to m...

I presumed was the traditional
eggnog. That's a heavy breakfast for a fellow not yet awake,
but fun was fun, so I took a
goodly gulp. Before I
swallow the stuff
explosi...

through with
coveries. The
vegetable dy
wife s...

CORNWALL BRIDGE, Conn.
COLLECTORS are snobs and
prudes. If they weren't prein-
diced, they would all be
old-fashioned s...

Elston of the c...
was enou...
now...

...ou THINK

IT MAKES *you* THINK by Eric SLOANE

AMERICANA

OF COURSE, humor is a dif-
...thing to define because it
...with time and circ...

"THERE S
ing to comp
of wit." say
Terwilliger of

MY F...

IT MAKES *you* THINK by Eric SLOANE

I'M

IT MAKES *you* THINK by Eric SLOANE

MAKES *you* THINK by SLO...

CORNWALL BRIDGE, Conn.
WHILE RESEARCHING early
barns, a farmer told me of a huge
Vermont barn built for "two pack
of horses." Having never heard
of a pack of horses, I voiced the
...ndering if he hadn't

of rabbits, a down of hares and
a skulk of foxes. A team of oxen,
a stud of mares, a tribe of goats
a flock of sheep and a harrass
horses. A labor of moles, a clo...
der of cats and a shrewdness
of martins
apes. A richness of
...umes of ferrets, a cete of ba...

Alas, I
allelomimet
disease. It
copied som
fooling. It
Mencken
around on
out in Cinc
...to do but t...

painting and writing
...ld barns for quarter of a
...y, I thought I knew quite
...about that subject. But
...began a book about barns.
...y started learning.
...le, I thought
...was som...

and because the circle
sents a perfection
many of the
cul...

IT MAKES *you* THINK by Eric SLOAN

I recall when Girl Scout cookies were made by Girl Scouts.
They had a home...

bona fide fund-raisir

CORNWALL
I'VE DONE
letters this we
reason. The so
for a new lette
be known
Tho...
w...

NEWSPAPER

1
2
3

IT MAKES *you* THINK by Eric SLOAN

IT MAKES *you* THINK
Respectfully yours
Eric Sloane

...have always said "Seville, sed
...nting paints buses inarol!"
...news- mar trux."
...sanduxl"
...other ch...

...ial signs, the revolt
...unions, big
...os..

na.
sig
"ty
are
sign
grea
sel

ITM

MAKES *you* THINK SLO...

I were to name the most
...atic bit of Connecticut

sketch pad is to catch the be...
in the moods of the wond...

IT MAKES *you* THINK